The Triumphs of His Grace

The Triumphs of His Grace

A Spiritual Odyssey

DAVID L. McKENNA

RESOURCE *Publications* • Eugene, Oregon

THE TRIUMPHS OF HIS GRACE
A Spiritual Odyssey

Resource Publications
An Imprint of Wipf and Stock Publishers
199 W. 8th Ave., Suite 3
Eugene, OR 97401

www.wipfandstock.com

PAPERBACK ISBN: 978-1-6667-7368-2
HARDCOVER ISBN: 978-1-6667-7369-9
EBOOK ISBN: 978-1-6667-7370-5

VERSION NUMBER 051823

Contents

Meet the Author

I was born on May 5, 1929, the year of The Jazz Singer,
The Flapper and The Great Depression, to a bus driver
and a taxi-dancer in a forced and loveless marriage,
but *Grandma prayed and Grace prevailed.*
Thanks be to God!

Aknowledgments

In a very real sense, this book is the product of multiple authors. Over a period of years, colleagues and friends have read the text and made their recommendations. They include: Alec Hill, Steve Moore, Shirley Ort, Bud Austin, Don Argue, Greg Asimakoupoulos, David Goodnight, Kimberly Rupert, and Rob Nicholson as well as members of our family. Special thanks are reserved for our eldest son, Douglas McKenna, for his insistence that the book be published and to Sheila Lovell, my former Executive Assistant at Asbury Theological Seminary, who labored faithfully and effectively on the arduous task of copy editing and formatting. Nor can I forget Cec Tindall, Executive Assistant to the President at Seattle Pacific University, who did the original editing back in 1970 and Joyce King, Secretary to the President, who typed the original copy and remained my cheerleader even after we retired from the University. I dedicate this book to Cec and Joyce with gratitude for the memories of our ministry together.

David L. McKenna

Prologue

THIS IS MY STORY

To Be Read with Hope

And of His fulness we all have received,
and grace for grace.

JOHN 1:16

ARE YOU DISILLUSIONED WITH the Church, its leadership and even the Christian faith itself? If so, you are not alone. In every generation our disappointment is recycled. I know, because I have been into the depths of disillusion myself. Yet, the Church continues, leaders lead and faith persists. Why? Because God has given us the gift of His grace in jars of clay to show that "*all-surpassing power is from God and not of us.*" It is through the cracks in our jars of clay that we get glimpses of His grace at work in astounding ways.

I dare to tell my personal story of growing up holy under the demands of an autocratic leader in a holiness tabernacle. The jars of clay, both individual and institutional, are obvious. So are the cracks in the clay. Through those cracks we see the harsh reality of human nature exercising its might in contest with the all-surpassing power of God. But we also get glimpses of His grace at work. My experience in this crucible of clay called The Tabernacle may make you angry, amused or amazed. I only ask that you be open to the evidence that, out of His fullness, grace upon grace is at work to redeem us and make us whole.

David L. McKenna

Note: Out of respect for the persons and families who are part of my story, I identify only myself and my family by the last name. Permit me, also, the privilege of filling in the stories for which I have facts but not all of the details.

1

We're Marching to Zion

HIGH AND LIFTED UP, his tones filled The Tabernacle. Brother Dan preached like Billy Sunday and played the trombone like Tommy Dorsey. To me, a 10-year-old boy who hated church and piano lessons, he was my instant hero. To the crippled Body of Christ huddling together in the make-shift sanctuary of The Evangelistic Mission Tabernacle, he was our last hope.

His image alone exuded confidence—Brylcreemed black hair, Mafia-blue shirt, white silk tie, and blue serge suit served as resplendent accessories for the golden glitter of his slide trombone. For the first time in the forced march of my spiritual journey, I laid aside Sunday School comics, doodle pads, and unholy fantasies to be mesmerized by every movement of the Messianic figure who had responded to our plaintive call for a pastor.

At the dinner table that day, I had heard my father say that the elders of The Tabernacle would decide that night whether or not they wanted to invite Brother Dan to be our new pastor. That was less than half the question. Deep down, Dad confessed his doubt, "Will Brother Dan want us?"

Feeling the pain of our conflicted congregation, Brother Dan seized the moment. Without so much as a prelude or a prayer, the object of my attention sprang to center stage on our rough and ready chancel at the stroke of half-past seven. Tone from a golden throat and a golden bell brought the service to an instant climax.

"Praise God!" He prompted us. "If you aren't shoutin' 'HALLELUJAH!' when you hear this song, you are dead and the devil's got your tongue."

With that command, he kissed his lips into the trombone mouthpiece and pointed the slide heavenward as if to give God notice that he was ready to play. A swoop of the slide set the music in motion. Crisp and clean, staccato notes tumbled from the reflecting bell in a Sousa beat. Even I knew the upbeat chorus, word for word:

> *"We're marching to Zion,*
> *Beautiful, beautiful Zion,*
> *We're marching upward to Zion,*
> *The beautiful city of God."*

Obedient to the musical cue, my grandpa Mac left his seat in the "Aye-men" corner to walk, prance, and jig before the plank-and-sawhorse altar of God. The wooden arc, curving across the front of the sanctuary, symbolized the center of worship for The Evangelistic Mission Tabernacle. When the faithful band of spiritual exiles had been driven from revival tent to storefront mission to basement sanctuary, they carried their altar with them. Only the sawdust was left behind.

Grandpa Mac's antics activated a second saint. Ratted or bunned, but always ginghamed, Sister Ida Mae was spirited out of her seat by the tug of raptured eyes and the pull of a hankied hand. She wept and waved, "Oh, Glory!...Glory!...GLORY!!"

No service went by without Grandpa Mac and Sister Ida Mae exchanging antiphonal shouts and rhythmical steps before the altar of God. Repetitious, but never boring, their performance warmed and lighted our worship in the damp and drab setting of our 20th-century catacomb. Need I add the obvious? The Evangelistic Mission Tabernacle stood across the street from a factory, next to a beer garden, and on the other side of the railroad tracks. Located in Ypsilanti, Michigan during WWII, it also had identity as the home for the Ford Aircraft Plant where B-24 bombers were made and the destination for countless numbers of Southern migrants who came to work on the assembly lines. Of course, they brought their culture with them in language, habits, social order, and religious fundamentalism with a charismatic flair. The Tabernacle served as perfect place for them to find social acceptance and a spiritual home.

My father and mother were no exception. In his mid-20s, my father, Loren McKenna, drove the Greyhound express between Detroit and Chicago. I can still see the picture of him in his bus driver's uniform, complete with a snappy-brimmed cap and knee-length leather boots. To make the non-stop trek the bus had a kitchen and the attention of a full-time steward. Dad's steward was an African-American man who also served as his best friend. If Grandma McKenna hadn't wanted her first grandchild to be David, my name would have been Samuel.

My father followed in the early footsteps of his father—a hard-driving and hard-drinking swashbuckler with an eye for gorgeous women. On his stopovers in Detroit, he frequented a dime-a-dance hall with its bevy of beauties. My mother, Ilmi and her sister, Limpi, had migrated from the quiet confines of their Finnish family home in Fitchburg, Massachusetts to follow the dream of being dancers in the Ziegfield Follies. In preparation for their entry into the wider world, Mom changed her name to Helen and her sister became Betty. Whatever happened to the Ziegfield auditions is lost in memory. One thing is certain. The sisters were far from home and stranded without income. As a last resort they opted for the meager earnings as taxi dancers in a dime-a-dance hall. It was on the dance floor that the destinies of my father and mother merged.

Out of reckless liaison, my mother became pregnant. Neither my father nor my mother was ready for marriage. Mom still had dreams of dancing in the Follies and Dad had no desire to give up the action at both ends of his bus trips. Family pressure, however, prevailed and a private ceremony was conducted by a Justice of the Peace. The date of the marriage is unknown, but the newly married couple moved to Ypsilanti and, thanks to Grandma's prayers, gave their hearts to Christ and became members of The Evangelistic Mission Tabernacle.

They arrived, however, just as dissension had severed the fragile seams of the poor and weak members of the Body of Christ who huddled together in their shabby setting for worship several times a week. At one time, their horizon had no limits. When the congregation first journeyed from the dilapidated storefront to the concrete bunker with its slit-eye casements, even the tarpaper bonnet that served as a temporary roof seemed to flap with the promise of a red-bricked and white-steepled sanctuary. Whatever others may have thought, for the handful of blue-collar folk who had imprinted every inch of mortar, every foot of lumber and every gallon of paint with their after-hours labor of love, the concrete block basement tabernacle had met their need for a spiritual home and symbolized their love for God's Holy House.

No longer. Flesh had so taken its toll on their spirit that the tattered tarpaper roof now slapped the sooty sides in hollow mockery of a lost dream.

The trouble began during the ministry of the founding pastor, Brother Ambrose, a long-suffering spirit who preached love, avoided decisions, and worked a full shift on the local assembly line. He had no choice, with a hellish wife, open-mouthed fledglings still in the nest, and a poverty-level congregation. In fact, it was his Lady MacBeth who did him in. Stirring her thirst for power into a cauldron of jealousy, she watched as the pot began to boil and bubble. One by one, innocent members of the congregation were alienated by Sister Eva, a red-headed circuit rider who indicted the men for mistreating her husband and the women for trying to seduce him.

For a time, Brother Ambrose tried to cover his wife's footsteps with apologies and prayers, but to no avail—the cancer had gone too far. By direct contact or contagion, every cell in the organism was infected. Finally, a meeting of the society was called to settle the issue. Brother Ambrose found himself pinched in a closing vise between his frau and his flock. Rather than fight, he resigned to become a spiritual exile in the Elba of a clapboard cottage that appeared to be sinking in a sea of weeds. Neighborhood kids soon concocted scary stories about the red-headed witch who lurked behind shaded windows and gobbled up children who failed to scream the shibboleth, "Witch, Witch" as they peddled furiously past the house.

Some years later, a fellow teen-age evangelist-to-be and I stormed the witch's castle behind a fusillade of prayer. Ex-Pastor Ambrose answered our knock and hesitantly, but graciously, invited us into the sparse and lifeless prison of his living room.

For an opener, I stuttered the words, "We . . . We . . . We came to tell you that we have been saved and are called to preach."

Brother Ambrose answered with the smile of a person whose life might not be futile after all. At least, his silence gave us the courage to on.

"God has given us a burden for . . . Oh, it's not that we think you're backslidden or anything . . . It's just that we would like to see you come back to church and preach again. Will you let us pray for you?"

Before the last syllable had tumbled from my lips, the room was shaken by the roar of a tornado with frizzy red hair, a wrinkled, chalky face, and blazing green eyes. "Get out . . . Get out . . . GET OUT . . . OUT . . . OUT . . . OUT!"

A human storm raged on the winds of flying hands and kicking feet. Sister Eva had made her debut. Unbeknownst to us, she had caught every word at her listening post behind the living room door. Each of our pleading words had fanned the coals of her smoldering hate and then, when I asked for prayer, all the flames of hell broke loose.

Shocked to our feet and pushed toward the door by her wrath, one of us stammered, "G- G-G-God bless you, Sister E-E-Eva," The other nodded farewell to the forlorn minister cowering on the couch.

Milliseconds later, two badly-shaken Christian martyrs scurried down the street, hurrying away from the scene of their burning.

"Now I know what the devil looks like," my partner gulped.

"Yeah, if that is hell, I sure don't want to go there," I echoed. "Did you see the look on Brother Ambrose's face? She's got a Satanic spell on him."

That was our belated introduction to the woman we now called "Jezebel," a blazing inferno with a husband whose "Aye-men" still stuck in his throat. Years earlier, many others of The Evangelistic Mission Tabernacle had been scorched by the same wrath. So much so that their future now hung in a balance weighted toward despair and defeat.

Brother Dan's first sermon coincided with our last hope. "Turn with me to Romans 1:16. The Apostle Paul writes, *'I am not ashamed of the Gospel of Jesus Christ, for it is the power of God unto salvation.'*" No matter that the innuendos on "*not ashamed*" included a peacock's strut and "*power*" had a Machiavellian twist. Brother Dan was in full control.

Whether the preacher-on-trial possessed an intuitive understanding of group dynamics or a sermonic script written by the Holy Spirit, he struck resonant chords of hope for a socially disenfranchised and spiritually disheartened people. Pride was our first need and he knew it. "Bless God, every time I read these powerful words, I want to shout from the highest housetop, 'I AM NOT ASHAMED OF THE GOSPEL OF JESUS CHRIST-AH.'" (Whenever tempo and intensity broke through unseen barriers in his preaching, Brother Dan slipped into the guttural connectors of "ah" and "uh" after key words and major points.)

Unaccustomed to assertive sounds from their modest pulpit, only a few scattered "Aye-men's" piped like automatic reflexes from the corners.

"Why should we be ashamed?" Brother Dan asked his awestruck audience. "If we are the redeemed of the Lord-ah, what does the Scripture tell us to do-ah?"

For a moment, timidity and ignorance ruled as the master's eyes teased out a response. Silence hung in the air until a female voice, eager as a grade-schooler with the right answer, squeaked, "Let . . . the redeemed of the Lord . . . SAY SO!"

"Yes, Yes, O-O-Oh, Yes," The teacher rewarded his pupils with positive reinforcement.

"Do you know what it means to be redeemed-ah?" Before anyone could answer, he gestured his class into an imaginary cross-legged circle at his feet with a nostalgic invitation. "Let me tell you a story. A little boy got a scrap of wood, some leftover sticks, string, and piece of cloth to make himself a sailboat. He worked for hours, putting loving care into each part."

How did Brother Dan know that my Dad and I were building a sailboat together in our garage? I came to full attention. Boring religion had been raptured into real life and touched me where I lived.

The miracle worker went on. "When the work was done, the little boy was so proud of his beautiful boat that he hugged it to himself, saying, 'You're mine because I made you.'

"He could hardly wait until the day came when he could take it to the lake and try it out. Setting the boat afloat on the wind-brushed waters, he again saw that it was perfect. For hours, he watched it skim the surface in circles before the gentle breezes-ah . . . BUT THEN, a contrary wind came up, turned it off its course, and blew it out of sight. The little boy ran along the shore, trying to catch it, until he fell to the ground, exhausted and in tears."

By this time, everyone had forgotten the original question: "Do you know what it means to be redeemed?" Death and misery shrouded us again, but Brother Dan knew right where we were.

"For days, he was heartbroken, refusing to eat or do his homework, until one day, while shuffling his way toward school, he passed a pawnshop window." Perceiving that he had cast a ray of light into our gloom, the preacher paused to let the visual snapshot of the boy and the pawnshop develop fully in our minds. Once satisfied with the image, he set the scene into motion and spun the obvious into the spectacular.

"Out of the corner of his eye, he spotted a sail! Was it just a wishful thought or a figment of his imagination? NO . . . IT WAS HIS BOAT-AH! Racing inside (why is that little boys always 'race'; frilly little girls always 'skip'; tough men always 'plod'; and faithful women always 'kneel?'), he grabbed the sailboat and triumphantly announced to the shopkeeper, 'This is my boat. I made it.'"

"'It'll cost you two dollars,' the pawnbroker told him. Nothing the boy could say about building the boat with his own hands or losing it on the lake could change the merchant's mind.

'Two dollars or put it back into the window.'"

"Heartbroken once again, the boy had no choice but to put the sailboat back into the window. But he knew what he had to do. Racing down the street, with his eyes straight ahead and his jaw set like steel, he charged through the front door of his home-ah, raced upstairs-ah, broke open his piggybank-ah, and counted out two dollars from his meager lifetime savings-ah, and ran back as fast as he could to the pawnshop-ah. Red-faced and out of breath, the little boy opened his chubby fist, spread the coins on the counter-ah, and panted, 'Here's the money, mister. Now, can I have my boat?'"

"'Just a minute.' the shopkeeper tantalized him. One by one, he counted out the coins on the counter while the little boy wriggled from one foot to another. Eternity passed before the man finally conceded, 'Okay, it's yours.'"

"Can you imagine the joy of that little boy-ah? He raced to the window, picked up his boat, hugged it once again, and spoke to it, 'You are twice mine now-ah . . . Once because I made you-ah . . . and once because I bought you-ah!'"

"Now . . . beloved, do you see what it means to be redeemed-ah? Once we were made in the image of God-ah . . . Praise the Lord . . . We were His and He loved us. But one day, we set the sails of our soul-ah to catch the winds of Satan-ah . . . and we were swept away from God to be lost in the sea of sin. BUT—PRAISE GOD . . . I SAY PRAISE GOD-AH! HE NEVER STOPPED LOVING US. He never stopped searching for us. Then, one day He found us on the shelf in the devil's pawnshop-ah. The price was too high . . . Satan refused to give us back our souls. ONLY THE PRECIOUS BLOOD OF JESUS CHRIST COULD BUY US BACK-AH."

"Bless the Lord. He paid the price for us. . .He redeemed us. . .and now we are twice His. . .Once because He MADE us, and once because He BOUGHT us. Ohhh . . . Hallelujah!!

"HAL . . . LAY . . . LOO . . . YAH! ARE WE THE REDEEMED OF THE LORD?"

Self-doubts vanished in a spontaneous chorus of echoing "AYE-MEN'S" and heads bobbed, "YES." For the first time in years at The Evangelical Mission Tabernacle, the redeemed of the Lord were saying so. As for me, a 10-year-old boy who loved sailing, I had received the first, most fundamental and unforgettable lesson in Christian theology.

2

There's Power in the Blood

BROTHER DAN BASKED IN the glory of his shining hour. Lifting his trombone and high-stepping around the pulpit, he brought his hearers to their feet with a triumphal shout, "ARE WE ASHAMED OF THE GOSPEL OF JESUS CHRIST?"

"NO, NO, NO!" was the unanimous vote.

"Then, let us SING-AH and SHOUT-AH the praises of our wonderful Lord wherever we go . . . In church ("Aye-men!") . . . at home ("Oh, Yes!") . . . and on the street ("Praise the Lord!").

Grandpa Mac pranced at the front and Sister Ida Mae pirouetted in the aisle. Emotions that had been plugged for months and years broke loose in the congregation. Even my father, a cool and collected spirit, raised his hand half a notch and emitted a quiet "Aye-men."

King Dan let his newfound subjects have their rein. Playing his trombone again, he blatted out in Basin Street style:

> *"There is power, power, wonder working power,*
> *In the blood, of the Lamb.*
> *There is power, power, wonder working power,*
> *In the precious blood of the Lamb."*

Everyone sang and some marched. Up the aisle, across the platform, and down the sides, a processional of unseemly saints snake-danced around us. Our dungeon flamed with light. But, just before the Spirit took full control, Brother Dan tooted his parade to a halt. After all, his sermon had a second point.

Leaning forward, squinting his eyes, and cupping his mouth, the preacher shifted into a conspiratorial tone. "Listen," he rasped like a spy passing on classified information, "it is the dead sinners and cold churches that should hide in shame. This town is filled with church tombstones built over the bodies of dead congregations. They may have the form of godliness, but we . . . we . . . we have the SPIRIT-AH . . . WE are ALIVE-AH . . . Bless God-ah . . . We are REDEEMED-AH! And as long as God gives us breath-ah, this church will shout Paul's message all over this city . . . I AM NOT ASHAMED OF THE GOSPEL OF JESUS CHRIST-AH!"

Brother Dan might have stopped right there. Instead, he went on to propose a rhetorical question as the second point in his sermon. "Why was Paul not ashamed of the Gospel of Jesus Christ? Because . . . it is the POWER of God-ah unto salvation."

Anyone who has ever read a sermon on "Power" knows what is coming next, but no one could anticipate the preacher's skill in making a worn-out illustration sound like a first-time truth from Mt. Sinai. Creating a scholarly image by pinching his knitted brow and burring his preaching tones, he articulated: "In the original Greek, the word for power is *dunamis*, from which we get our word 'dynamite.'"

Quickly, as if he did not want to overextend the intelligence of his listeners, Brother Dan slipped out of the scholar's mask and back into his cornpone style. "Ah learned 'bout dynamite when ah was a boy on the farm. Grandpappy was buildin' an irrigation ditch to water the crops. He had to blast through some rock to free a stream, so he went into town and brought back a box of dynamite. Then, he drilled holes in the center of this heah-old rock-ah, put the sticks of dynamite into those holes . . . and-uh . . . when everything was set, he struck a match to the fuse. Ah was just a tad of a boy, but ah remember the fire catchin' the fuse and fuzzin' along the line. Grandpappy knocked me down and fell on top of me. VAARRR—ROOOM!!!"

To accompany his sound effects, Brother Dan mimicked the explosion with the body language of hands mushrooming upward until he stood on tiptoe. Suspended there for a dramatic moment, his hands then curled downward like a settling atomic cloud.

He went on. "Our eardrums almost split as we choked on the smoke and dirt in the air-ah . . . but when I looked up-ah . . . the rock was split wide-open and the stream was runnin' through! PRAISE GOD! OH, PRAISE GOD! 'Man, that's power,' you say, but it is nothin' compared to the power of God-ah. If we let Him, He will put a stick of His spiritual dynamite into a crack in our stony heart . . . by the fire of His Holy Spirit-ah. .. . . . light our fuse-ah . . . and blast away the hardness of our souls so that the streams of livin' water can flow through-ah . . . flow through-ah . . . flow through . . . GLORY TO GOD-AH!"

Before we could savor that promise, an unseen hand passed over Brother Dan's put-on, farm-boy face and left behind the piercing eyes and thrusting jaw of an angry prophet. "There are some hard hearts here tonight-ah . . . that need to be melted . . . No, no, not melted, but BLASTED . . . by God's holy dynamite-ah. Some of you haven't cracked a smile since I began preachin'. You-ahh . . . are squirmin' under conviction and you know it. Right now . . . right now . . . right now God is trying to get a stick of dynamite into a crack in your stony soul, your hard heart. Others of you have hardenin' of the spiritual arteries. God's life-givin' stream has been dammed up by sin and reduced to a trickle." (Preachers have a way of saying "dammed" that would be considered profanity in any other context).

"Aye-mens" were now reduced to a trickle. Sensing a kill on his cornered prey, Brother Dan bayed like a hound and struck for the jugular. "The Word of God that you've heard preached tonight has become a stick of dynamite in your soul. Now, I say-ah . . . let the FIRE fall . . . let the BLAST be heard . . . let the stony hearts be BROKEN . . . LET THE LIVING WATERS FLOW-AHHH!"

His voice almost broke under the decibels of a hoarse shout, which prompted me to look up and spot a well-studied crack in the ceiling. I fully expected it to split open under the power of falling fire and gushing water. Instead, as the preacher's hands settled slowly downward from the top of his last point, he brought down the first leaden sense of guilt upon my 10-year-old soul. Condemnation by the freight load chugged through my mind. "I stole a dime off my mother's dresser yesterday . . . I said 'Damn it' last week . . . I smoked my first cigarette last summer . . . Woe is me. I am the sinner he's preaching about—hard, dry, stony and hopelessly lost."

If Brother Dan had given his altar call at that moment, his first convert would have been a bawling 10-year-old kid who had just received the title "Chiefest of Sinners." But two points do not a sermon make, so after a well-timed pause, Brother Dan cut through the humid air of guilt with the anticlimax of his sermonic triad. "Thirdly, and in conclusion, the Apostle Paul says that he is not ashamed of the Gospel of Jesus Christ: for it is the power-ah of God unto salvation to EVERYONE-AH THAT BELIEVETH, to the Jew first, and also to the Greek. Praise the Lord, that means YOU" (a searching index finger traced a course of manifest destiny across the congregation with periodic stops on troubled faces) ". . . and YOU . . . and YOU . . . and YOU!"

Marching to the cadence of some distant drumbeat, the withering finger of justice moved toward me. I scooched and shrank, ducked and dodged, certain that my sins would be fully exposed by the bionic eye and guillotine finger of the anointed Man of God.

" . . . and YOU . . . "

Here it comes.

" . . . and YOU-AH . . . "

The finger of judgment hung over my head.

" . . . and YYOOUU!"

HE MISSED ME!!

Just as the blade of doom was slicing down upon me, Brother Dan spun on the heel of his patent leather shoes and slashed sideways as if to pick up any leftovers he had missed in the first sweep.

Whew! Relief was quicker than Bufferin. Why? Why had I escaped? A misshapen and gerrymandered childhood theology came to my rescue. During the two-week revival that had been billed as an old-fashioned camp meeting last summer, the evangelist had preached on The Age of Accountability. Using a subtle twist and an unwarranted generalization about Jesus' encounter with the scholars in the Temple at the age of twelve, he contended that all children below the age of twelve would go to heaven if they died. BUT, when you reach your twelfth birthday, it is "ZAP!!" if you don't repent.

"That's it," I reasoned ever so smugly, "Even though I've sinned, they don't count for two more years." So, with my sins annulled and my guilt deferred, I smugly hummed through seven verses of:

> *Just as I am, without one plea,*
> *But that Thy blood was shed for me;*
> *And that Thou biddest me come to Thee,*
> *O Lamb of God, I come, I come.*

While humming, I turned around to cast the eye of judgment on those who needed it and settled back to watch sinners, twelve years and older, bump down at the mourner's bench to have their fuses lighted and their hearts exploded so that streams of living water could begin to flow.

How they came and how they prayed—sobbing as if they were already damned, praying, "O God, I'm a sinner." Their pleas were accompanied by sopranos sing-songing scripture and basses intoning, "Yes, Lord" with occasional groans of exhaustion providing punctuation for the discordant sounds.

Striding behind the altar and among the kneelers was Brother Dan—coat off, tie askew, black locks pasted by sweat to his brow, but still the General-in-Command with an uncanny sense of timing. Like a Godsend, he appeared among the repenting sinners during a frustrating lull, bent down to whisper some holy promise into their ears, placed his hand upon their rumpled heads, and gave the order, "Let's pray." Lighting the fuse of prayer once again, only seconds passed before the explosion came in the cheers that Brother Dan led, "Bless God . . . Oh, Hallelujah . . . Praise His name-ah . . . He has come!"

More often than not, the sinner looked up for the first time to smile through a red-blotched, tear-streaked face, "Oh, Yes, Lord, I do believe." Heated prayer and explosive shouts then gave way to tender song,

> "*I do believe,*
> *I do believe,*
> *That Jesus died for me;*
> *And that He shed His precious blood,*
> *From sin to set me free.*"

To climax this claim on salvation, Brother Dan usually took the hands of the soon-to-be-born again, lifted them skyward, and offered a soothing final invitation, "Won't you claim His promise and take Him by faith tonight? Just say, 'Jesus saves me now.'"

Obediently, the invitation was accepted when the convert spoke the words of relief, "Oh yes. Yes . . . I do believe . . . Jesus saves me now."

With that, a new spiritual creation was ushered into the Kingdom of God by another round of shouts and songs. Brother Dan? He had more work to do. Savoring the scene of a new birth for just a moment, he moved on to his next delivery.

When all had prayed "clear through," they testified publicly about their passage from death to life, along with whatever confessions, restitutions and prayer requests they had (even if embarrassing). The service concluded three hours after it began with a full show of hands waving to the rhythm:

> *When we all get to heaven,*
> *What a day of rejoicing that will be!*
> *When we all see Jesus,*
> *We'll sing and shout the victory!*

Concurrent with the sound of the last "Aye-men" of the benediction, Dad wrapped my hand in his and led me to the front of an impromptu receiving line to welcome Brother Dan. I hung back as

Dad said, "Brother Dan, God sent you to us. Will you stay and be our pastor?"

My new hero smiled affirmatively, but answered politically, "If it is the Lord's will."

A gentle nudge then thrust me forward into the presence of greatness. Dad said, "This is my son, David. He wants to play the trombone, too."

For the first time, I noticed the circles of sweat under the armpits of the preacher's Mafia-blue shirt. He was human! No matter. God's giant knelt down on the platform to even up our eyeballs, extended a dripping palm, and made himself God again by speaking to me as if the two of us were all alone in the world. "That's great. And are you going to be a preacher, too?"

Dazzled and dignified, I spoke an eternal vow at that spot between the altar and the pulpit. "Yes, sir." It was enough. I was spirited away, repeating my pledge to be a Gospel preacher and a trombone player just like Brother Dan.

Shortly after that, I took my first trombone lesson, but I had to wait two more years before I could repent in a style fit for a future preacher.

3

Out of the Miry Clay

A GODLY HERITAGE IS often spawned in the miry clay. If my spiritual history were ever staged as a musical drama, the overture would have to be the Gospel song that the saints of The Evangelistic Mission Tabernacle sang as they sobbed:

> *He bro't me out of the miry clay,*
> *He set my feet on the rock to stay;*
> *He put a song in my heart today,*
> *A song of praise, hallelujah!*

Charles McKenna or "Grandpa Mac" as I always knew him, started out life as a scoundrel of sorts. No one knows for sure why he and a passel of younger brothers were orphaned by their parents at an early age. Except for the name McKenna, almost all of their roots were cut and lost. As Grandpa Mac used to tell me the story, the only traces of his tattered ancestry were the etchings on an Irish Whiskey bottle and a faint recollection of a great, great grandmother with the Irish name of Bridget O'Toole Shannon of County Cork.

Blarney aside, the only known roots for the genealogical tree of the McKenna clan sprout from a forbidding Roman Catholic orphanage that held down the earth on a Midwestern flatland.

Grandpa Mac's visual memory of his hated homestead was the conflicting image of the heavenly spire with the cross on top standing out in sharp relief against the formidable gray stone walls of the spiritual fortress. Inside, punishment and purity were forged into a chain of discipline that shocked the spirit of a 12-year-old boy who had already grown old as the foraging father for a family of waifs.

Like Oliver Twist, it was just a matter of time before he broke for the streets, determined to make the money to buy freedom for the four McKennas he left behind. A lie about his age, a curse to prove his manhood, and stubbornness against pain soon earned him a place among the hod-carriers on a construction gang. From there, his practical intelligence and ambitious discontent vaulted him into machines, engineering, and finally, tool and die making. Job to job, town to town, he hopscotched across the Midwest, wooing a short-term wife and siring a son. By the time he met my grandmother-to-be, he was fortyish—a skilled, but itinerate craftsman, an irresistible ladies' man, and an inveterate liar.

Quite in contrast, Miss Cora modeled the petite image of her melodious French name. When Charles blew into her small Midwestern town, she was tatting hats in the local millinery shop. Was it Fate or Providence that brought a cigar-chomping, bar-hopping Jim Dandy into union with the innocent designer of fashionable ladies' hats?

As was his custom, Charles scouted his new town of Van Wert, Ohio, for the beauties worthy of his favor. Cora hardly fit the bill for his typical conquest, but sometime during his sidewalk survey, he spied the wisp of a woman whose aristocratic features were framed through the flowers of the hats in the store window. Mustering his choicest bits of palaver and spitting down his wayward front-lock, Charles glided into the shop, doffed his summer straw, and with the air of a country gentleman, won an invitation to tea. From then on, it was easy. A choice young maiden who had been too shy for the first spin of the marriage-go-round was wooed and subdued by the mature master of masculine wiles.

If Grandpa McKenna's winning style was played backward in the days of his courtship, his strategy would have been deceptively simple.

"Excuse me, ma'am" would be his open gambit, followed by some justification for his presence in a ladies' hat shop, "But I am a visitor in your fair city. If you had only a few days to spend here, what places of cultural interest would you want to see?"

Miss Cora must have been too absorbed in the question to note the betrayal of mechanic's grease around the moon of his fingernails. Charles had guessed right. Her knowledge of the subject broke her shyness and she jumped to answer his question with all of the confidence of a tour guide for the Chamber of Commerce.

"You only have a few days? . . . Umm . . . I would start with the historical museum around the corner. Exhibits there trace the history of our town back to the Indian tribe that camped along the river. Out by the mill, for instance, you can still find the Indian artifacts if you know where to dig."

Charles nodded his head to the rhythm of his intentions. He encouraged Cora to speed on.

"Oh yes, don't miss the exhibit in the side room of the museum. It shows that our town was settled by pioneers who had a taste for the art and architecture of the Old World. Even today, if you drive down Front Street, you can see some of the frescoes and motifs that the Stewart and Hayden families from Europe used to dignify their homes. In fact, some of Mrs. Stewart's original oil paintings in the style of Monet are still in the lobby of the oldest building in town. See that bank across the street?"

"Frescoes," "motifs," and "Monets"—Charles was sinking in the quicksand of his own question. In borderline panic, he scrambled for the firm ground of getting his animated bird to talk about herself.

"Now I know who does the beautiful designs on those hats. You are an artist! Tell me, how do you do it?"

A blush travelled upward from Cora's neck to her eyes as he put out the bait of a compliment. His exuberance caused Cora to shift her eyes to the back room to see if the owner was watching.

An unruffled curtain without that familiar eye glaring through a small opening dared her to take the bait.

"Oh, it's nothing. I sew in the morning and sell in the afternoon."

Charles saw his angle of approach. "You mean that you don't even have time for tea?"

"Oh yes," she apologized, "I get thirty minutes for lunch, but often work 'til tea time."

His strategy worked to perfection. "Say . . . tomorrow morning, I want to spend some time in the museum. I'm sure that I'll come away with some questions. If I come back at tea time tomorrow, will you help me out?"

Oh, to be needed—not for beauty, not for wealth, not for sex, but for knowledge! Cora bubbled in effervescence, missing the subtle sound of emphasis in her new-found suitor's words — "spend time in the museum." One step in and one step out qualified for the truth for foxy Charles, who later told me that he went through Harvard, in one door and out the other.

"Well, I don't know . . . You see . . . "

Back-room curtains blew apart to reveal the stony face and x-ray eyes of the high-bunned, stiff-corseted matron of the shop. Rather than withering under the glare, Cora's sleight-of-hand responded instantly with a wit that would later prove to be more than a match for Charles'. Nervous fingers were already tracing the brim of a hat on the counter, so that all she had to do was raise it along with her best sales voice.

"Why don't you think about this overnight, sir, and come back tomorrow afternoon? I'm sure that you'll decide to BUY it."

"How kind of you, ma'am. Business will keep me until the afternoon, but you can be sure that I'll be back. Yes, I'm quite sure that this is the hat I want." Turning to the baffled store owner, who was torn between a scolding and a sale, he defused her ire with a compliment. "Ma'am, I travel all over the world and have yet to find such beautiful hats or such gracious service as I have received in your store today. Thank you and good afternoon."

Two devastated women were left in his wake. One had met her match; the other had met her man.

Tea, museum, carriage, millpond, picnic, proposal, engagement, and marriage—Grandpa Charles was forty-two years old with no time to waste and Grandma Cora was twenty-four and counting. Alas, that's where the trouble began. Grandpa Mac, never one to tell the truth when a lie worked better, had presented himself as a patient bachelor of twenty-eight who was just waiting for the right woman to come along. Not until the marriage was consummated and the first baby conceived did Grandpa shock his second wife with the facts of his past life. Whether in a moment of weakness or rage, he blurted out the truth, "I'm divorced and once a father."

Grandma McKenna needed years to recover. As a selective Bible student, she unequivocally believed Luke 16:18: *Whosoever putteth away his wife, and marrieth another, committeth adultery; and whosoever marrieth her that is put away from her husband committeth adultery.* Transposing the "hims" and "hers," Grandma concluded that she was living in adultery. No matter that Grandpa was divorced, not an adulterer, she simply reasoned that the Scripture gives only one ground for divorce. Because Grandpa was not divorced on these grounds, he was still married to his first wife. Ergo! To live with a married man is to live in adultery.

Feelings of sin weigh just as much as sin itself. Grandma slumped spiritually under that load for years. Turning inwardly to dwell with her guilt, she became a self-taught student of the Word of God. Her bondage then turned into her freedom. Through the study of the Scriptures, she confronted the literacy of the opposite truth, *"If the Son therefore shall make you free, you shall be free indeed." (John 8:36)*

As an impressionable youngster, I labeled those words as "Grandma's verse." Her natural inclination toward theology had led her to choose Grace over Law. Deep down, those reservations might have remained. If so, they never surfaced before me. Before her grandson she lived as a forgiven and free spirit.

Despite her confusion over divorce, Grandma McKenna was, in the classification of William James, a "healthy soul." Always tender of conscience, sensitive to people and reverent toward God, she grew into her faith without the trauma of an earth-shaking struggle stamped by a precise time and place. Among the folks at The Evangelistic Mission Tabernacle, this was a handicap. Spiritual status seemed to be directly enhanced by the depth of sin from which you were dramatically delivered with a New Birth date for annual celebrations. Traveling evangelists who advertised "From Prison to Pulpit" or "From Witchcraft to Jesus" were the envy of those of us who tried to compete with conversion from stealing apples to smoking cornsilk.

Grandma McKenna never let her handicap bother her because Grandpa McKenna had all of the credentials for William James' "sick soul." By the time he was converted, almost sixty years of flagrant sins were behind him. A distorted idea of Roman Catholicism had served as his eternal shield and buckler. Without so much as a nod toward The Church since his escape from the orphanage, he counted on his Baptism to cover one end of his life and Final Absolution the other. Grandpa McKenna was long past signing a creed or returning to Mass for his salvation. His spiritual history demanded a radical, life-changing upheaval.

Like Saul of Tarsus' ride on the Damascus road, Grandpa McKenna's journey toward salvation began as a routine trip. Andrew, a gentle, self-effacing man who worked beside him in the tool-and-die shop, started him on the way. Natural magnetism drew the two craftsmen together. Over their lunch buckets and on the long walk home, Grandpa noted that Andrew smiled when other men cursed. Intrigued by this sign of joy, Grandpa's curiosity became his undoing.

"What makes you different?" he asked.

Simply and without pretense, his friend answered, "Jesus."

Grandpa quickly donned a sterile mask for protection against the infectious name. To him, Jesus meant the iron-fisted authority of the crucifix on the wall of the Roman Catholic orphanage or the severe God-man who had almost ruined his second marriage by

His pronouncements on divorce. Nothing more was said, but as Grandpa Mac testified later, "God put a hook in my jaw."

A Bible served as the barb. Andrew always carried a New Testament in his lunch bucket for reading during lunch break.

"What are you reading?" Grandpa blurted out one day before he could coordinate his tongue with his sight of the black leatherette cover with the gold letters, "HOLY BIBLE."

If Andrew had just answered, "The Bible," another "Oh!' might have worked. Instead, the Cross outflanked him by invoking that cursed name again. "I'm reading about Jesus."

Grandpa fought back with a curse, "Dammit, what's He ever done for you? For me, He's only trouble."

His bench partner raised his head from reading to speak peace into the brewing storm.

"I know what you mean. Jesus was only trouble for me, too. I thought that He took the fun out of life with His ideas about sin and hell—particularly after my wife got saved. She turned out to be a better wife, but it sure ruined our night life."

Grandpa lapsed into silence, allowing his partner to go on,

"One day, I started reading the Bible in order to win arguments with her. Wouldn't you know it, I lost another argument when I found out that Jesus came to forgive us our sins, not to send us to Hell. Then I went another step. The more I read, the more I realized that Jesus really enjoyed life, not the overnight stuff that cracks your head in the morning, but the true joy of sins forgiven along with the hope of eternal life. Do you understand, Mac?"

"No. Is that why you are always singing at the bench?"

"Hmm. I didn't realize that I did, but yeah, that's why."

Andrew played out the line and Grandpa McKenna ran again. But not far. Soon he was sneaking a Bible into the basement or the bathroom for a short snort with this Jesus guy. Cautiously, and usually with an edge of skepticism, he risked more and more questions with Andrew until one day they were seen together thumbing through the Bible during the lunch break.

Grandpa McKenna was now ready to be reeled in. His Bible-reading at lunch contradicted his curses at the bench, his boozing with the boys, and his trademark of a black cigar. On the narrows between heaven and hell, he had to go one way or the other.

Andrew aided his decision. "Why not come to church with me next Sunday night?"

"No, the walls would cave in."

"No pressure . . . anytime you want to go, let me know."

Still remembering the severe warnings of the priest against attendance at Protestant services, Grandpa knit his brow and queried: "What-a-ya-do there?"

"Oh, sing some of the songs that I've been humming, read the Bible, and listen to the preacher talk about Jesus."

"Is that all? Do I have to confess? Would I know what to do?"

"Sure you would." Andrew judiciously avoided the question about confession from his Roman Catholic friend.

"O.K. Maybe I'll go sometime." Grandpa always knew when to hedge his bets.

Only Grandpa McKenna himself can tell the rest of the story. After his conversion he never missed a chance to tell anyone he met how he was born again through the blood of Jesus Christ. Whether at prayer meeting, Sunday worship, evangelistic rally, street meeting, or on the banks of the Huron River where he fished, every kid knew Grandpa's testimony by heart.

Brother Dan always allowed time in the services for testimonies. With the invitation came the caution about making it a "popcorn testimony"—pop up, speak up and sit down—so that everyone would have a chance. Grandpa Mac only heard "testimony" and turned off his hearing aid. Instantaneously, he was on his feet awaiting his turn. Others always had priority, even those who stood up late, but Grandpa's shining face and nodding head cheered them on.

Eventually, his turn came. Facing the congregation from his self-appointed "Aye-men" corner, he rocked from heel to toe in rhythm with his recitation. "I want to report victory in my soul. On October 28, 1925, I came through the doors of this church as the Chiefest of Sinners.

"Oh, if you asked me, I would have told you that I was a no-good Catholic who hoped to work his way through purgatory, but the truth is that my sins were so many and deep that I was bound for hell. I lied, I cheated, I drank, I smoked, I swore—you name it, I did it."

He paused to let his sins blacken and deepen in the imaginations of his listeners. To add to the effect, he began to pace three or four steps along the path of the altar, head down in shame, and up in contrition. Suddenly, with the timing of an accomplished dramatist, he pulled up short, threw both hands into the air and shouted, "THEN JESUS CAME, OH PRAISE HIS HOLY NAME! 'Charles McKenna,' Jesus said, 'Come unto me, I'll forgive your sins and set you free.' THAT WAS IT. I ran down the old sawdust trail, and bumped my head against this old-fashioned mourner's bench and prayed cle-ear through to VICTORY. OH, HALLELUYAH, HAL—LAY—LOOOO—YAH!!!"

His red-tipped cane tapped out a triumphal march across the front of the sanctuary, up the aisle, around the back, and down to his seat again. Gnarled hand waving in the air, cataract-filled eyes glistening with tears, and ancient feet shuffling in rhythm, he always closed with the spiritual song of his own composition:

Oh, I lost them on Calvary's hill,
I lost them on Calvary's hill.
I remember the night
When they rolled out of sight,
Oh, I lost them on Calvary's hill.

I am sure that Grandpa Mac never read Pilgrim's Progress. Yet, like Christian, whose burden rolled off his back when he knelt at the cross, Charles McKenna, too, had fallen before that tree and turned to watch his sins roll down, down, down and out of sight.

Grandpa Mac sang his song one Sunday night and died two days later. A man on welfare leaves no inheritance, but my legacy is full. He bequeathed to me the "shush" of a fishing trip, the expertise of making willow whistles, the image of a shouting saint, and the song of his redemption. Along with those gifts, he left me one last verse of Scripture that he drew out of the promise box at the Tuesday morning prayer meeting the day he died. Was it just coincidence that I picked at random the same promise during family devotions the day after his funeral:

The Lord shall preserve
Thy going out and thy coming in
From this day forth,
And even for evermore.

Psalm 121:8

From scoundrel to saint, from miry clay to solid rock, Grandpa McKenna left me a good and godly heritage.

4

Search Me, O God

EVER SINCE THE NIGHT that Brother Dan blessed me with the touch of his hand, I determined to play the trombone and preach the Gospel. By the time that I reached the age of twelve, half the dream had come true. I was a promising trombonist and an accomplished liar.

Like the trombone, lying takes practice. Under the cover of my faulty logic about twelve as "The Age of Accountability," I tried some rousing sins—inhaling cigarette smoke, spitting cuss words, betting pennies on 500 rummy, and funding my ventures with periodic dips into the coffee can that contained the Sunday offerings for The Evangelistic Mission Tabernacle. Of course, all of these amateur sins required professional lies—an art that I had mastered.

Even today, I am hard-pressed to imagine the web of deception that I wove with an 11- year-old mind in order to skip school and attend a movie matinee all alone. Kids in my fifth-grade class whetted my appetite for the forbidden fruit by making the laughs of the Laurel and Hardy comedy that was playing at the Wuerth Theatre an "inside joke" among those who had seen the movie. My frustration at being left out peaked when they told me that film finished its run on Wednesday. Zero Hour was just two days away.

It was now or never. My parents used to give me dimes for the Western Saturday matinees, but never, never could I attend movies on school nights. There was no hope . . . unless . . . filaments of fantasy began to spin into a web of deception.

Money was no problem. A stealthy side trip through my father's den, coupled with a momentary stop at the coffee can, produced the price for admission and a bag of popcorn. The next day, then, I made sure that all of the routines for attending school were acted out, including the synchronized timing of a fond farewell. Then, with unusual precision I greeted my fifth-grade teacher listlessly, "Good morning, ma'am." When she did a double-take to inquire about my health, I chortled inside over the easy unfolding of my Perfect Crime.

Shortly after the lunch hour, the final strand of my scheme fell into place. Sacrificing the fun of recess, I stayed in the room with my head down on the desk. Sure enough, my teacher missed me and returned early to sympathize with the plight of her model student. Pressing her pre-chilled hand against my pre-heated forehead, she presented her diagnosis. "You might have a fever. Let me send you to the nurse."

"Oh, no, ma'am," I protested, "My mother told me to come home if I didn't get better."

"Do you want to leave?"

"No, ma'am. I don't want to, but maybe I'd better . . . maybe if I go to bed this afternoon, I can come back to school tomorrow."

As innocent as a fly in flight, she hit the sticky web. "Why don't you go home, then? I'll understand."

With one more feverish sweep of my hand, I relented, "Yes, 'um. I think I should."

Gathering up my books as a pretense for doing homework if I had a rapid recovery, I walked out of the room and schoolhouse with the disguised air of a prisoner who escaped jail through the warden's office. Out the oak door, down the marble steps, through the green signal light, past the blue-uniformed firemen who always loitered on the mirrored fenders of their red engines, I headed on the path to home. Two more blocks took me out of the line of sight for school eyes so that I could slip sideways into the back alleys leading uptown.

Fear stabbed at my guilty heart when I passed a stranger. Was he a truant officer? Did she wonder what an 11-year-old was doing on the streets during school hours? As much as possible, I stayed in alleys and on side streets until I surfaced at the four corners in the center of town.

The Wuerth Theater anchored the block of stores on my right. Black letters on the flashing marquee spelled out "LAUREL AND HARDY COMEDY." Although I now preferred some high adventure to match the daring of my own exploits, I heard again the laughs of my chums on the playground as they extolled the film. So, I stepped up to the ticket window and counted out the stolen coins for the price of a theater ticket. Luckily, the woman behind the bars responded like a vending machine who cared nothing about my size, age or presence during school hours. Likewise, the doorman blankly tore my ticket in half without so much as a look of recognition. Instinct told me that neither of them could be the manager. He was the one I feared.

Inside the lobby, I faced another dilemma. To the right were stairs, to the left was an aisle. Which way would I go? Is it safer in the balcony or on the main floor? I opted for the balcony and, once upstairs, sighed in relief at the view of a hundred empty seats from which to choose. What fortune! As I settled into a front and center seat, I marveled at the power of the practiced lie.

Laurel and Hardy played to me alone. Having missed the credits and the opening scene, I arrived just in time to see a tin can tossed up, up, and up until it landed in precarious balance on the top of a pile of discarded cans that pyramided high against the sky. The camera then panned downward until it settled upon two leftover soldiers in a trench eating beans with knives. The skinny one was Laurel, the fat one was Hardy—sad sacks of World War I who had never heard the news that the Armistice had been signed many years ago. I relished every slapstick moment, including the classic scene of Laurel sitting without pretense in a wheelchair with one leg under him. Hardy assumes that his old war buddy has suffered an amputation and sympathetically wheels him all over the Army base. Upon Hardy's invitation to go for a ride in his new car, however, Laurel quickly unfolds his leg and walks away from the wheelchair. The bopping begins—not only for Laurel, but for me. Hushed voices descended from the stairs behind me.

"Oh, oh," I thought, "The manager called the police." But no, when I chanced a peripheral glance, there were just two men debating the selection of their seats. I relaxed and returned to the antics on the screen.

My two unknown compatriots sat three rows behind me and up to the right. As usual, they had to catch up with the film by second-guessing the thinly-veiled plot. Semi-hushed whispers distracted me so that I heard every syllable. Otherwise, I might have missed the incriminating accusation aimed at me after their pupils adjusted to the darkness. One of them spotted the small silhouette of my head in the front row. "Shouldn't that kid be in school?"

Verbal shock hit my ears and ricocheted through my mind. All of the guilt that I had so smugly repressed moments earlier erupted in a volcano of molten fear. Scooching down in the seat, the movie was over for me. What if they were policemen? Did they know my principal? Would they go to the manager?

"ESCAPE" obsessed me; hysteria paralyzed me. My frenzy was broken only when the dim light of the theater fell into darkness as a night scene was projected on the screen. MY CHANCE! In a startled reaction, I was up and gone, fully expecting a giant claw to jerk me to a halt. Yet, I retained my composure long enough to vault down the stairs of the balcony and break free into the red-velveted walls of the upper lobby.

Down the stairs again, I picked up speed, decelerated through the lower lobby, left-faced at the door of the theater, and clung to the edges of the stores along my escape route. Not until I reached the main intersection did I muster the courage to sneak a backward look. WHEW! The streets were clear and so was I. With a moment to reflect upon the nature of judgment, I recalled my mother's frequent admonition, "Be sure your sin will find you out."

No one had found me except my conscience. "When I am twelve," I thought, "I'll have to take care of this."

Guilty or not, I decided that it was safer to practice the slide trombone. With five years of piano lessons already notched in my musical belt, Dad and Mother eagerly signed the permission slip for trombone lessons at school. The next day, I appeared at the door of our home with a battered black case housing a silver trombone with a dinged bell and a sticky slide. No matter. Driven by divine motivation, I practiced obsessively and progressed so rapidly that I was soon playing first chair trombone ahead of sixth graders in the elementary school band. My golden moment came that spring when the conductor invited me to advance early into the junior high band. His glossy introduction marked the acme of my musical career. "David will be our next Glenn Miller. His tone is the best I have ever heard from a young player." From then on, my career as a trombonist was all downhill. Inspiration from Brother Dan made me an early achiever, but sooner or later, the heart for music must be matched by the ear for music. I had the heart, but no ear.

****

In just a little more than two years, Brother Dan had rallied the spirits and hands of his motley flock to build a steepled church of colonial style on top of the tarpapered pillbox that he had inherited. My father, who transmitted to me his love for New England, designed the structure. Red brick, white trim, columned entrance, and stub-pointed cupola complete with a bell transported a bit of ersatz Massachusetts into a Midwestern setting next to a coal yard and across from the railroad tracks. Inside, the décor shifted between the colonial simplicity of the walls, windows, ceiling, and lights and the theatrical decadence of second-hand, snap-up theater seats and a massive performing stage over which Jesus presided in a wall mural of the Second Coming.

The stage itself was divided between the orchestra and the choir. Another division was created by the pleated, maroon velvet vanity curtain that not only clocked the angle of wandering male eyes when women sat on the platform, but also separated the preacher from the people. Circling gently along the same arc as the vanity curtain, but on the floor, was a solid oak altar, at least forty feet long, sufficient to hold thirty or forty sinners on the front side and a double row of praying saints on the back side. Many times, the number would multiply when repentant souls made an altar of front seats and their intercessors knelt in double and triple rows between the seats and the altar.

Front and center on the platform, where the vanity curtain had a tempting gap, stood the massive oak pulpit, designed and constructed by my father for the preaching of the Word. On the front side were the jig-sawed and hand-carved letters spelling out "*Worship the Lord in the Beauty of Holiness*," a constant reminder for preaching the doctrine of Entire Sanctification as a second work of grace.

Looking back, now, I see the magnificent style of the colonial architecture as a symbol of the contradiction with which I wrestled. How do I reconcile the classic image of a colonial church with the tent-meeting mentality that dominated the services? Today, I see that contradiction as evidence of my case. On the auspicious occasion of the dedication service, I proudly took my place on the front row of the orchestra, between a plowboy saxophonist and a playboy trumpeter. A red-face clarinetist who was shaped like a Buddha filled out the front row. In front of us was the grand piano, an ebony, second-hand Steinway over which Sister Alma, Brother Dan's wife, presided. Behind us plucked two guitars and a banjo. Their beat was accented by the tuneless thumps of the bass drummer and the misplaced "oom-pa-pa" of a tuba player.

Without prior practice, Sister Alma led us into the prelude, "Onward, Christian Soldiers" hoping that her husband's brilliant trombone would wipe out the dissonance. I alone, among the brass and reed players, had no ear for music. Sooner or later, in every service, spontaneous songs and choruses replaced the notes on the music stand. Brother Dan would turn to his wife, announce the key, and away they would go—all except me. My greater embarrassment was still to come. When the band fell into step behind

Brother Dan for a parade around the Tabernacle and blatted out, "When the Saints Come Marching In," I sat all alone in my seat searching for the notes. Others testified that the Holy Spirit gave them the gift of music. For some reason, He missed me.

5

A New Name in Glory

As expected, I crossed my spiritual Rubicon at the age of twelve. Following the Tabernacle's rite of passage, I was promoted from the Children's Department to the Young People's Society on the Sunday after my twelfth birthday. Membership meant the obligation to add a six o'clock Sunday evening young people's meeting to a Sabbath already intolerably long. As with most youth programs of that era, adolescents hung in the suspension of a spiritual "No-man's Land." Activities for the young were limited to mini-evangelistic rallies or upgraded show-and-tell testimony times. Youth ministers did not exist, so beleaguered volunteers exhausted their imaginations on program ideas to compete with the allure of the world for the souls of the young. And, of course, a whole passel of parents accompanied their children to the service.

I was born again through the induced labor of a gimmicky young people's meeting shortly after my twelfth birthday. In imitation of the Wednesday night prayer meeting, my Aunt Colleen, Young People's Superintendent, led a testimony meeting one Sunday evening. Our place was in the old cellar sanctuary of the Tabernacle, now repainted and curtained, but still damp and drab. Slatted benches that corduroyed your bottom still served as pews and two-by-twelves notched over sawhorses still functioned as the basement mourners' bench. Scores of Tabernacle-ites marked spots on the makeshift altar where they had been saved, sanctified, and, oh so often, reborn again and again.

Every conceivable device had been tried to enliven the testimony time for the young people. "Popcorn" testimonies—pop up, praise the Lord, and pop-down—were famous, but overworked. "I want five people over thirty and five people under twenty to testify" had also run its course. So, Aunt Colleen, stretching her creativity, announced, "Tonight. . . we are going to do something different and exciting. We will testify according to the alphabet. When I call an 'A' everyone who has a testimony and a last name that begins with 'A,' stand up. Then we'll go to 'B,' then 'C,' and on down through the alphabet until we finish with 'Zs.' Do you ever know anyone whose name began with a 'Z'?"

Under his breath, I heard the resident skeptic of the back-row gang whisper hoarsely,

"Ain't she ever heard of Zorro?" Irreverent chuckles provoked a stern and puzzled look from Aunt Colleen, but she contained herself and plowed on with all of the suspenseful aplomb of a Bingo operator calling out numbers,

Six little Allens all stood in a row. Their father, Brother Allen, fit the image of a hen-pecked husband—bald, bespectacled, and overdue for dentures. Sister Allen ruled over her husband and family with an iron hand. To see the two of them together was a comedy, but to imagine them at work on the production line in their bedroom strained the outer limits of comic relief. Nevertheless, six little tow-headed Allens, boys with home-hewn haircuts and girls in hand-me-down ginghams, stood full-dress in parade file and on Brother Allen's gummy nod, drew out giggles and "Bless God's" when the youngest lisped her testimony: "I'm thaved, thank-ti-fied, and on my way to heaven." Then, in the most unsaintly fashion, she spun on her mimicking brother to pronounce, "Tho. . .There. . .Too."

Six Allens later, Aunt Colleen called out, "'B'? Oh, we've got lots of 'Bs.'"

Unknowingly, Aunt Colleen had created a countdown to judgment for me. As each letter was called, everyone twisted and turned to identify all of the people in the company with a last name of the call-letter. When Bobby Barnes, the Zorro commentator, failed to stand with the "Bs" he drew the "Tsk, Tsk" look of a hundred convicting eyes. Silent harassment finally forced him to his feet for a mumbled testimony that barely passed muster with the grand jury, but for those of us who knew him best, we knew that he had lied through his teeth.

"C?" With the sound of the letter "C," "Conviction" came upon me. Never before had I been trapped in a situation where I had to declare my faith by forced choice. Playing in the Tabernacle band, reading Scripture during Bible study, and even mouthing a prayer in a Sunday School class — none of those had called my bluff.

"D?" The moment of truth had come. On my twelfth birthday I had crossed the timeline into The Age of Accountability. Just as Brother Dan predicted that all of our sins would pass before our eyes at the Last Judgment, a horror show of lies, stolen coins, and smuggled cigarettes flashed across the screen of my subliminal mind. Even Laurel and Hardy had lost their humorous touch. Burrowing deeper into my soul, I unearthed the same " . . . zoo of lust, nursery of fears, harem of hatred. . ." that caused C.S. Lewis to condemn his inner being as "Legion." I, too, possessed many devils.

"E?"

"F?"

"G?"

Each letter echoed from eternity. God and I were on a collision course from which there was no escape. Head pounding, heart heavy, mouth dry, and feet twitching, what would I do?

"H?"

"I?"

All of the grand strategies I had used to get out of trouble came and went. Stubbornness: "I'll just sit here." Deception: "I love Jesus and want to do His will." Flight: "How about a coughing spell for a quick exit"? Fantasy: "If I scooch down, maybe she won't see me."

I was a sinner in the hands of an angry God. Sweat dampened my armpits when I reran the nightmare of standing alone and exposed at the bar of the Last Judgment. Drilled by the piercing eyes of His righteousness, a voice like the roar of many waters sealed my condemnation. *"Depart from me, ye wicked one. I never knew you."*

"K?" . . . No Ks?"

"Let's go to the Ls."

Just before the brush of a holy finger swept me to the left and into a herd of goats headed for Hell, my inner spirit screamed, "Oh God, I am guilty. . .Jesus save me!" God answered through a distant voice that shocked me out of my haunting reverie:

"M?"

Was it true? Did I still have a chance? Dad stood immediately to lead the McKennas in testimony. Grandpa Mac wasn't there that night, so Grandma Mac followed. (As noted earlier, membership in the Young People's Society began at twelve, but had no age limit because Christ kept the oldsters "young at heart.")

Now Mother. . .now Sister Pat.

No more M's—EXCEPT ME! I was a spiritual wreck, drawn and quartered by a burning conscience and a tortured imagination. I tasted the acrid smoke and felt the searing coals of a bed in Hell. Tension pushed beyond tolerable limits when Aunt Colleen acknowledged my turn with a tender smile and just waited for me to stand.

ENOUGH!!! Hands that betrayed my age by the last traces of baby fat grabbed for the top slat of the bench in front of me and pulled me to my feet. Somewhere from deep in my soul, an alien voice broke past my shredded pride to declare: "I NEED TO PRAY!"

Automatic reflexes turned my feet toward the aisle. In the background, sobs and shouts sent heaven the signal that a sinner was coming home. Earth and its downward pull upon me were almost lost, except for the "S'cuse me" that I muttered when I stepped on a lady's toe while trying to get to the outer aisle.

Never, never, never will I lose sight of the face that met me when I reached the altar rail. As I found out later, the second I said, "I need to pray," my Dad bolted from his seat on the center aisle as if he were the repentant soul. But no, he went straight through the opening between the sawhorses, turned to the right, knelt down, and waited inside the rail to welcome his son. Our eyes met to open a floodgate of tears that neither of us had ever known before. Our arms locked in a vow of eternal love and our knees buckled down in a mingling of human and divine love.

Contrary to all of the formulas for forgiveness, I did not pray. There was no need. Confession was complete when I dared to say, "I need to pray" and conversion was accomplished through the "Forgive me's" that I prayed on the path to the altar.

So, in the symbol of father's arms, my soul was taken into the bosom of the heavenly Father. There, I sobbed myself into exhaustion and then rested in the peace of knowing that my sins were forgiven.

****

Each passing year adds value to the experience of being reborn in my father's arms. For one thing, I worshipped him. Early in our relationship, I remember the gift that he brought home for me during the Depression after he had lost his office job and had to resort to loading boxcars at the local Ford assembly plant. Coming home one winter evening, he put my five-year-old frame on his lap and announced a surprise in his lunchbox. Prying its snap-locks open, I found a black, hard-rubber disc with a hole in the middle. It was a rubber washer used as a shock absorber between automobile engines and the boxcar floor during shipment. As I curiously turned it over and over, Dad spoke with the creative pride of the poor, "I didn't have the money to buy you a hockey puck, but I thought that this might do." He made me the captain of stick-games on ice.

Later on, Dad had to take a job out-of-town. Saturdays belonged to me and Sundays belonged to God. Together, we built a sailboat for the local doctor and flew model airplanes. Only once do I remember his patience with me fraying. While steaming the hundreds of thin strips that made up the smooth-flowing hull of the racing sloop, I abandoned my post at the end of the steaming barrel, ruined several strips, and drew a Franklinesque lecture that began, "*A job begun is a job half done.*" That's the way it should be with a father and son who are buddies and friends.

Still later, an accidental revelation of Dad's pre-Christian life taught me the meaning of conversion. During a McKenna family reunion at Thanksgiving, entertainment for the men was offered at a new pool table in the basement. According to the law of The Evangelistic Mission Tabernacle, pool tables and bowling alleys were taboo—instruments of the Devil himself.

Perhaps that is why the pool table intrigued me so much. Feigning righteousness by standing a reproving distance from the table while my non-Christian uncles, Mark and Milan, were playing, I studied the game with envy. From time to time during the merry-go-round of changing positions to get their shots, an uncle would stop to coax me, "Wanna play?" Consistently I shook my head "No" while nursing the silent hope that I would be asked again.

A three-cushion shot ended the game with Uncle Mark the winner. In his exuberance, he turned to me with the invitation, "Here, Dave . . . let me show how a winner does it."

I accepted. Uncle Mark wrapped himself around me to maneuver my hands, fingers and eyes into a pool-shooting posture. I shot—twice, three times—losing awkwardness and gaining accuracy with practice. Concentrating on my introduction to a forbidden joy, I lost track of the people around me until I was stabbed awake by a familiar, authoritative voice, "Here, son, let me show you how to do it."

Dad, from whom I expected reproof, took down a cue from the rack, chalked its tip with an expert twist, test-glided the stick through his left finger, and with only a casual aim, Englished a ball into the far pocket. Ball after ball disappeared from the table, cushion shots caromed once and twice before finding their target, and a behind-the-back trick shot missed by only a fraction.

"Dave, you may not know it, but your father used to be the best pool-shark in town."

My hero was human! Slowly, his history leaked out. Leaving high school before graduating, Dad found his lot with the rowdy crowd that frequented pool halls. Adventure lured him to the big city. There, he floated from job to job until his wanderlust was channeled into a bus driver. In the groupies around the bus station in Detroit, Dad met a dime-a-dance girl who eventually became my mother. Once or twice, I had thought about the parallel between Grandpa McKenna's scalawag days and Dad's exploits when they testified about the depth of sin from which they had been rescued. Thank God, twelve-year-old minds are like twelve-year-old bodies—innocent of the coming trauma. For me, I only knew that the man who welcomed me at the altar in my twelfth year was a friend with whom I had shared many good things. Conversion—a 180-degree turn from the past life — was now one of personal understanding.

****

The rest of the young people's service that night was anticlimactic. Rising from the altar, my swollen eyes fought to focus on the faces around me. Grandma McKenna, Mother, Sister, Aunt Colleen, Brother Dan—Everyone! Hugs and handshakes, smiles and shouts, songs and sobs, signaled my grand entrance into the Kingdom of God. Aunt Colleen stood as the guardian at the gate,

"Ms are still up, David. We've been waiting for you."

I was ready. Grandma McKenna pushed a fresh and dry handkerchief into my hand as I stood among intercessors who were still kneeling, squatting and sitting around the altar. "I've played Christian for a long time . . . (tears began to flow again) . . . I've cheated, lied, and stolen . . . (more tears) . . . I've got a lot of things to make right . . . but, tonight . . . I know . . . I KNOW THAT JESUS SAVES ME!"

I fell back into my father's arms amid a flurry of soggy handkerchiefs and spitty hallelujahs. Joining with my father on earth and my Father in heaven, I knew the joy of one lost soul coming home.

Whatever else happened that night is lost in the treasured memory of the postscript to my new birth. After church, we piled into our pre-war Plymouth with the "A" gas rationing sticker on the windshield. My new status in the family became obvious when Mother pushed down the rider's seat in the front of the two-door sedan and climbed into the back seat with my little sister. I had been promoted to the trusted position of co-pilot for the car. Two blocks from The Tabernacle, I was still savoring my spot in the front seat, with its luminous dials and oncoming lights, when Dad began to sing,

> *"I was once a sinner, but I came*
> *Pardon to receive from my Lord. . .*
> (Mother picked up the verse with him)
> *. . .This was freely given, and I found*
> *That He always kept His word. . ."*

Having already learned the tune on the trombone, I joined the jubilant duo,

"There's a new name written down in glory. . ."

Dad and Mom stopped. It was time for my solo. On or off-key, I sang the song of the Born Again,

". . .And it's mine. . .
Oh, Yes, it's mine!"

Theologians may fault the theology of the words and musicians may cringe at the quality of the tune, but they cannot contest the personal meaning of the song for me. "*There's a New Name Written Down in Glory*" has a niche in my hymnody alongside Charles Wesley's "*O for a Thousand Tongues*" and Bach's "*All Glory, Laud and Honor*."

6

Love Divine, All Loves Excelling

ALMOST 20 YEARS AFTER my conversion, I needed all of the reserve strength that I could muster from the memory of my redemption at the age of twelve. Again, it was Dad and me. I was now at Spring Arbor College as president, the youngest college president in the nation and on the brink of my inauguration. The event was especially anticipated because George Romney, Governor of Michigan, would give the address. It was to be a proud moment for the McKenna clan, led by my father.

A phone call from Dad a couple months before the inauguration changed my life forever. With a coldness I had not known before, Dad asked me to meet him at a restaurant parking lot on the road outside of town. The same face that had given me a tender welcome across the plank of a saw-horse altar was now an iron mask across the hood of an automobile. With one slash of a verbal knife, Dad cut the cord that had bound us together in love for so many years. "I am going to divorce your mother."

After a decade of shouting matches, separate bedrooms, and sullen lapses into hostile silence, his words were no surprise. I had a question to ask; "Is it true that another woman is involved?" My question was the first salvo over the chasm of our broken relationship. I spoke, not as a son to his father; I spoke as man-to-man.

"Yes." His response was flat and factual.

Perhaps to protect myself, I had no further questions about "Who?" and "When?" Instead, my thoughts rushed back to the most cherished moment of my life when Dad welcomed me at the altar. Words from a reservoir of emotion erupted: "But Dad, what about Christ?"

Surprise blinked in his eyes. Dad paused as if he too remembered the altar scene. But then, a curtain of case-hardened steel slammed down on whatever traces of regret were left. Someone other than my father answered: "I never knew Him."

Even in denial, Dad had chosen the words of Peter's betrayal. It was too much for me.

"I don't believe you! What about the time that you met me at the altar?" Stirred-up memories seethed to the surface. "What about the time when we prayed about my call to preach? What about the time . . . ?"

Like a traffic cop on the corner, Dad raised his hand to signal "STOP." "I never believed any of that. I was a victim of social pressure. In fact, I only professed religion because of you kids. Otherwise, I would have left your mother long ago."

A cheap shot, but not as cheap as the one to follow. "I have never told you, David. . .but I didn't want to marry your mother in the first place. Do you know why we never let you know the date of our wedding anniversary?" (I had suspected, but now I knew). "Your mother was pregnant with you and we had to get married."

Bitterness toward my father was introduced as a new emotion for me. "Do you mean to say that I am illegitimate?"

"No," he protested, "You were made legitimate by the marriage, but it wasn't because of love."

Heredity had endowed me with steel to match steel. "Dad, you can't hurt me now. I am my own man. I have my own faith. I have my own family. I can stand on my own two feet."

Without shaking hands, we walked away from each other—a walk that did not end until two weeks before Dad's sudden death.

Twelve years went by. I was now president of Seattle Pacific College, soon to be University. We were planning our oldest son's marriage and struggling with the question of whether or not to bring my estranged parents to the ceremony. Before we made our decision, Dad called and asked if he could come with his wife. The call further compounded my dilemma because Mom had just been diagnosed with leukemia and been given nine months to live. In the hardest decision I have ever made, I called my Dad back to tell him "No." Because Mom had such a short time to live, I told my father, "Dad, this is Mom's day. I will do nothing to spoil it."

The wedding justified my decision. Mom's face glowed as she sat in the aisle seat of the second row and witnessed her oldest grandson being married. She even rallied her strength and took Debra, our oldest daughter, up to Paradise on Mount Rainier. But, not long after she returned home, the leukemia sapped her strength, crippled her right leg, and left her hobbling as she walked. I felt compelled to visit her again and take her to dinner. Knowing her love for New England, I blew the budget and ordered her a Maine lobster.

When the dish arrived, Mom said, "Oh, I can never eat all that" and then proceeded to clean her plate. Afterward, I drove her to the Wednesday night prayer meeting in the Free Methodist Church. I can never forget the last time I saw Mom alive. With her head up and her back straight, she negotiated the three steps up to the doors of the church by obeying the doctor's recommendation, "Good leg up, bad leg down." Within weeks, Mom died and I spoke at her funeral using the subject "From Taxi-dancer to Saint of God." She earned the title by her grit and received the title by His grace.

Two years later, our oldest daughter was to be married. Mom died exactly nine months after our son's wedding and I still felt justified with my decision to tell Dad, "No." Now, however, it was time for reconciliation. I gave him a call with the invitation to come to the wedding at our expense. Dad responded instantly with acceptance and our conversation turned into a preview of all of the joys ahead. At the end, I found the grace to end our strained separation of fifteen years with the words that I needed to say and he needed to hear: "Dad, I love you."

Little did I know that I had pronounced a benediction between us. One week later, Dad suffered a massive stroke that left him in a vegetative state. Because of my administrative duties I had to take a red-eye flight to his bedside in Sarasota, Florida. At a three-hour, nighttime stopover in Chicago I wandered through the empty concourses. A yellow paper cut out in the shape of a satchel caught my eye and curiosity caused me to pick it up and open it. Inside I found only the words of Psalm 121, the McKenna Psalm. I could only gasp. Never before had God spoken so clearly to me. My grandpa, father and I were bonded together in the promise of God *"preserving our going out and our coming in, henceforth and forever more."* (Ps 121:8)

When I arrived at the hospital in Sarasota, I saw only the remnant of a man I knew and loved. Dad's eyes stared off into space, froth appeared on his lips and he uttered meaningless sounds. The faith that I had mustered for the moment disappeared and I kicked the wall in defiance of God. Untimely death took away any chance to rebuild our relationship on the foundation of restored love.

God got the blame and took the brunt of my bitterness.

WHY? Just when redemptive love was strong again.

WHY? Just when I could show my sons where I got my love for them.

WHY? Just when I had admitted how much I needed my dad.

God heard me out. Slowly, He put the pieces back together. His first move was to bring back to consciousness a preacher's story that I had heard many times.

A father had lost his only son to tragic death. Boiling with bitterness, he made a close Christian friend the scapegoat for his anger, "Where was God when my son died?" he raged. God spoke back through the inspired calm of his friend who answered, "The same place He was when His own Son died."

Steeled eyes over the hood of an automobile still hurt me, but they no longer cancel out the tender, tear-filled look that welcomed me to a sawhorse altar. I looked at my father again and saw the stubble of a two-or-three-day growth of beard. To be unshaven violated my father's sense of well-being. In a flashback I remembered the Christmas when Dad received his first electric razor as a gift from Mom. Sheer delight filled his eyes as he tried it out right in front of us. On impulse, then, I opened the drawer of the hospital cart, and there it was! Dad's electric razor. As my gift of love and through a flood of tears, I shaved my father's face for the last time. Then, in my final act, I took the tract that I had found at O'Hare Field, opened it to the words of Psalm 121, and pinned it on the bed over Dad's head for all to see. As I left the room and headed back to the airport, one thought possessed me. When my father and I meet again, I will begin where we left off,

"Dad, I love you."

7

I Love to Tell the Story

One by one, the dominoes fell on my call to preach the Gospel. Brother Dan had tipped the two-spot domino when he blessed me with the touch of his hand and the incantation of his words, "God wants you to be a preacher."

Almost three years passed before the second domino fell. Then, click, click, click . . . the falling pieces gathered momentum. For the first time, I attended to the facts as well as the feelings of Brother Dan's sermons. Imitating my father's habit, margin notes began to appear in my Bible. Next to Matthew 25, for instance, I wrote in ink on the India paper with the reference: Brother Dan "Sheep and Goats" 1/15/43.

Later on, my note-taking matured into outline form as I secretly stored up texts, topics and "firstlys, secondlys and thirdlys" for future sermons. More than once, the messages I heard were reproached with slashing gestures and silent shouts before a self-imaged congregation of one in the reflection of my bathroom mirror.

My "Let's Pretend" sermons chain-reacted against another domino. Brother Dan had to move over and make room for other heroes in my self-styled Hall of Fame for preachers. In the never-ending processional of visiting evangelists who traipsed across The

Tabernacle platform, several served as transient models for me. I say "transient" because each of them eventually fell from their exalted position with crumbly feet of clay.

Envy, more than admiration, drew my attention to "Little David," a 12-year-old evangelist who was billed in civic auditoriums, tabernacles, and revival tents as a "Child Prodigy Anointed by God to Win America for Christ." If he could preach to the acclaim of thousands, why couldn't I? Grand visions danced in my head as I imagined countless multitudes crowding out a big-top to await my message.

Then, my moment came. "Little David" himself was scheduled for an all-city, one-night stand at the county fairgrounds. I had to meet my competition, assured that once we shared our mutual passion for preaching, he and I would become history's first tandem 12-year-old evangelistic team. Carefully, I laid my plans to persuade my father to take me to the rally without Brother Dan's knowledge.

Subterfuge was necessary because Brother Dan neither allowed nor admitted competition. A Tabernacle-ite who was discovered sneaking away to a revival meeting of any other church, even on the off-nights between prayer meetings and evangelistic rallies, was scorched in the next Sunday's sermon. So, when Brother Dan read that "Little David" was to preach at the fairgrounds, he publicly ridiculed the rally as a "spiritual side-show in the Devil's own territory."

Coincidence spared me the risk of confrontation. Two weeks before the rally, while I was gathering courage to ask my parents to go, Life magazine featured "Little David" in pictures. One look and my envy evaporated. "Little David" was not at all what I had imagined! Curly, golden locks tousled around his baby face, ruffled satin cuffs and collar accented his velvet suit, and silver buckles topped his black, patent leather shoes. Instantaneously, "Little David" became nothing more than a detestable Buster Brown, Peter Pan, Bobby Shaftoe, and Little Lord Fauntleroy packaged as a preaching prodigy. If this was the price for preaching the Gospel to the millions, I wanted none of it. Mentally, a red pencil crossed "Little David" off my list.

Next came 20-year-old Brother Charlie. What a contrast with "Little David." Cornstalk legs hinged his bottom half together and cornsilk hair sprouted on the unhinged upper half of his six-foot-four frame. His scarecrow body topped off with a Huck Finn face complete with fiery freckles and crooked teeth. Broomsticks for arms and legs would have given his clothes a better fit. He had the neck of a famished turtle, the hand of a wasted cadaver, and the feet of a circus clown. In his own way, Brother Charlie was fresh and living proof that God cares more about the heart's intent than the body's appearance.

All of the disparate parts of Brother Charlie clanked together when he picked up his "gee-tar," plucked out some rollicking country Gospel tune, and sang with the toothy, nasal drawl of a self-taught preacher.

Brother Charlie was a split-second celebrity with the Tabernacle crowd. Peppering his sermons with double negatives, split infinitives, dangling participles and intentional fractures of Yankee English, Brother Charlie made hay with his handicaps. I admired him because he showed God's promise for a young man who obeyed the call to preach.

Our ways parted during Brother Charlie's third time around as a Tabernacle revivalist. In the first two meetings he had high-jumped the vanity curtain, landed on the oaken altar, broke into a dead run around the Tabernacle, and ended up using the altar on the opposite side as a starting block to hurdle the vanity curtain once again—just in time to announce the "secondly" and "thirdly" of his unlettered discourse. What else could he do? I soon found out.

In the middle of a sermonic tirade, he accused his audience of falling asleep and losing the Holy Spirit. A green Gospel song book magically appeared in his hand, and before anyone could duck, it became a missile flung in a flurry over the bug-eyed heads of his captive congregation. Just as the song book fluttered like a wounded bird into the lap of old Sister Morgan, Brother Charlie buried his freckled nose into the pages of the huge pulpit Bible. All that was visible was the violent burrowing of his disheveled head ripping up leaf after leaf of the Holy Word. Full shock at this borderline blasphemy had hardly hit before his head snapped up on the pivots of two inflamed eyes coupled with the raging command, "When the Spee-rit moves, Y'all must obey God!!"

Quicker than a shutter's flash, he cleared the vanity curtain once again, grazed the altar and tight-roped over the backs of refinished theater seats, racing with miraculous ease across the hazardous inch-wide toeholds of narrow uprights, dodging deftly on an obstacle course between the heads of gaping worshippers, and thumping down without incident on the aisle at the back. Brother Charlie's race course now took him at full, long-legged gallop across the back of the Tabernacle and down the right-hand aisle to the space in front of the altar. His Grand Finale was to turn cartwheel after cartwheel before the altar of God. I can still see his sweat-matted, cornsilk head go down and his broomstick legs come up to form a Ferris wheel turning over and over again. No doubt about it, Brother Charlie's congregation was now wide-awake, but he lost his niche in my pantheon of preaching heroes. Not only were the pages of the Bible sacred to me, but I always fell side-ways whenever I tried to turn cartwheels.

One by one, my Holy Heroes fell. Brother Jimmy, a maverick Nazarene, scraped and gouged for every trace of carnal pride with the burr-edged tool of a caustic tongue in order to live up to his advanced billing as "The Nation's Greatest Holiness Preacher." Masochism had to be the motive that paralyzed us when he dug past our sinful pride into human dignity and self-consciousness. For a 13-year-old boy who couldn't fathom the meaning of "Eradication" or "Perfect Love," Brother Jimmy plummeted from his pinnacle as a preacher when he pronounced our modest sanctuary "too nice" for holy people. To prove his point, he lowered his shoulder into the top of the heavy, oak pulpit and heaved it from the platform to smash, bounce, and splinter against the matching oak altar.

Most of the Tabernacle-ites went wild in the presence of a fallen idol, but I noticed that my father neither smirked nor smiled.

After all, he had fashioned that pulpit as a labor of love, not as a monument of pride. To see it smashed by a preacher's pique under the guise of holiness preaching should have called out a question of honor and invited a duel for the truth.

Instead, my dad said nothing. After the service, he helped the men replace the pulpit to its prominent position in the center of the platform. Fortunately, oak against oak had caused limited damage, but both pulpit and altar carried the scars of Jimmy Miller's preaching for the rest of their days. Perhaps the greatest damage was symbolized by the effect of the fall upon the jig-sawed and hand-carved verse of Scripture that stood out on the front of the pulpit: "WORSHP THE LORD" . . . remained intact, but " . . . IN THE BEAUTY OF HOLINESS" had several bruised or broken letters. Service after service, I stared at those letters. Resentment swelled up within me when I remembered watching Dad give every letter an artistic touch and tender care. Brother Jimmy came close to making me deny the doctrine because I saw nothing holy in his act.

"Little David," Brother Charlie, and Brother Jimmy caused me to be disillusioned with preachers, but it did not dissuade me from preaching. I continued to jump through all of the hoops that I judged to be essential to a man of the cloth—early morning prayer, daily Bible reading, faithful church attendance, and a readiness to "preach, pray or die." One hoop eluded me. Each preacher who came to town recounted the miracle of their calling:

God spoke in flaming tongues. . .

God stopped them in their sinful tracks. . .

God knocked them from their horse. . .

God opened up the skies.

Gentle persuasion was not enough. Without a vivid portrayal of a personal encounter with God, the credentials of my calling were deficient. My anxiety was further heightened by an evangelist's story. Recounting the special anointing that God reserves for His ministers, the evangelist told of a stammering soul who sought God's will for his career following conversion. His prayer was answered one day as he was planting corn in the field.

Startled by a bright light he looked up to see a supernatural sign in the sky that read, "GO, P.C." The simpleton instantly interpreted "Preach Christ" in the letters and began to follow the call down a path of utter failure. Finally, in desperation, he sought spiritual counsel from a senior minister who was willing to hear his story. Assessing the natural gifts and verbal skills of his counselee, his mentor came to a conclusion: "The letters were right and the call was clear," he reasoned. "Only your interpretation is wrong. God called you, not to 'Go, Preach Christ,' but 'Go, Plant Corn.'"

Perhaps, I too had misinterpreted God's call. Serious soul that I was, a new period of searching prayer began. A few days later, God indulged my need for a sign, not sky-borne letters, but with the poetic words of a prophet's call. During one of my youthful vigils of watchful prayer and progressive Bible study, all of the lights of heaven came on when I read Romans 10:14–15:

> *"How shall they hear without a preacher?*
> *And how shall they preach, except they be sent?*
> *How beautiful are the feet of them that preach*
> *the gospel of peace."*

God had given those words for me:

Hear . . .

Sent . . .

Preacher . . .

Beautiful feet . . .

Gospel of Peace.

Not a doubt remained. Compulsive power pressed down upon me until I knew what the Apostle Paul meant when he cried, "*. . . woe unto me if I preach not the gospel.*" (1 Cor. 9:16). Without reluctance, I accepted God's charge and immediately sensed the weight of an onerous command being lifted and replaced by the buoyancy of lighthearted joy. Thus, I learned both sides of God's promise. Like a first-time ambassador with a new portfolio under my arm, I tripped off on beautiful feet into a future that promised to be filled with the glad tidings of the Gospel of Peace.

At the next opportunity I recounted my experience in the congregation of faith, fully expecting a joyous demonstration followed by a news conference. Nothing of the sort took place. For sure, Brother Dan led a few cheers on my behalf, but basically the response came off in the "So, what else is new?" category. Brothers and sisters who met me at the door patted me on the head and spoke a common word, "I knew all along that God wanted you to be a preacher." To me, the call was a supernatural breakthrough; to them, it was a natural sequence.

Brother Dan did not wait long to test my calling. Occasionally, he permitted parts of our services to be dedicated to "Amateur Night"—non-singers led the singing, non-readers stumbled through the Scripture, and non-preachers expounded on a Biblical text. For some reason, Brother Dan chose to break me in as a song leader in Wednesday evening prayer service. Flattery and my newly-minted call overcame common sense, so I accepted.

Mimicry tooled my arsenal. For a short lifetime, I had watched song leaders exercise the authority of calling out page numbers, nod to the orchestra for an uneven attack on introductory notes, and wave their arms to the intuitive beat of a built-in metronome. Even if I were tone-deaf and rhythmically spastic, success was guaranteed. Once you started the Tabernacle-ites on a Gospel tune, a song-leader became superfluous. Sheer momentum carried the song through to the ragged end. But ah, at the critical juncture between songs, the leader could win immortality through the medium of witty sermonettes. Most often, I had heard pithy little take-offs on the hymn of the moment. "The Old Rugged Cross" became the text for three-point moralizing on "Rugged" and "I'm Dwelling in Beulah Land" created the topography for a trip from the slums to the Heavenly City.

When my turn came, I stayed true to form. A finger-walk through the index of Tabernacle Hymns stopped early in the alphabet on an old-timer:

> *"Amazing Grace!*
> *How sweet the sound,*
> *That saved a wretch like me.*

I once was lost,
But now I'm found,
Was blind, but now I see."

With inspired, infallible and inerrant confidence, I displayed my 13-year-old intellect to an untutored congregation. Smugly, I announced: "John Newton was sitting under an apple tree one day. An apple fell and hit him on the head. That was how he discovered the Law of Gravity . . . Praise the Lord! But that was nothing compared to his discovery of 'Amazing Grace' when God saved his soul . . . Hallelujah!!! Let's sing together Hymn Number 294, 'Amazing Grace.'"

At the end of the hymn, I left the platform in triumph and took a seat next to Grandma in the congregation. Guffaws were about to burst through the laughing wrinkles around her eyes as she leaned over to me and whispered: "Isaac Newton discovered gravity; it was John Newton who wrote the hymn."

Mortification set in. I who had been dramatically called to preach the Gospel had committed a *faux pas* of eternal consequences in my first trip to the pulpit. Surely, the Holy Spirit had abandoned me. So, convinced that God and I had miscommunicated about plowing corn rather than preaching the Gospel, I slumped into the seat to await the sermon from Brother Dan, a truly called and competent preacher of the Gospel.

Frankly, I remember nothing of his sermon until he used the pioneering spirit of Christopher Columbus as a prototype of Christian courage. How can I ever forget Brother Dan's error that out-blooped my Isaac Newton story? He was as confident as I had been cocky when he reported the historical fact: "Christopher Columbus sailed across the Atlantic Ocean and did not look back until his feet were firmly planted on Plymouth Rock."

What a cure for my depression! Just the summer before, our family had visited the Pilgrim colony and I had climbed down to the smelly, shelly rock called "Plymouth." Maybe I had mixed up my Newtons, but I could never mistake Columbus for the Pilgrims.

Grandma McKenna looked at me, I looked at Grandma McKenna, both of us barely containing our laughter. But alas, no one else picked up the cue, so the two of us could only communicate through a knowing bump of elbows while biting our tongues. Years later, Grandma and grandson still shared the secret of the *double faux pas*. Even when she was too weak to rise from a bed in a nursing home, her eyes twinkled with the playful humor of one last joke. To reduce the swelling ego of her grandson with a newly-minted PhD, she wondered aloud, "Let's see, Dr. McKenna, which Newton was it who landed on Plymouth Rock?"

8

'Tis Burning in My Soul

AFTER MY FAULTY SONG-LEADING experience, one final domino had to fall on my call to preach. Grandpa McKenna, now in his mid-80s, was being victimized by senility. Tracks of time could be traced in the clouded eyes, shortened steps, and dulled memory. Watching the aging process take its toll, my single thought was, "Grandpa must hear me preach before he dies."

Brother Dan, of course, had missed my revised version of Newtonian physics, and under no circumstances would he ever know the inside joke between Grandma Mac and me about his faulty knowledge of American history. As far as he was concerned, I had passed muster as a potential preacher with my prodigious insight into the history of the hymnody. So, in the closing days of my 13th year, Brother Dan invited me to preach as a special feature of the Wednesday evening prayer meeting. The notice was short. In fact, it happened on an impulse during the exit from a Sunday morning service. Brother Dan always coordinated a hand pump with a holy check. "Bless God, Brother Dave, how is it with your soul?"

Spiritual satisfaction oozed through my smiling response. "Praise the Lord, I've got the victory."

Lights blinked, wheels whirred, and bells rang in rhythm with the pastor's handshake.

"Sa-a-y-y, why don't you preach for us on Wednesday night?"

Months of secret preparation collapsed into three days. I hesitated. "Well, I don't know, that's not much time!"

Brother Dan's eyes shifted from the spontaneity of a personal invitation to the rigidity of a divine command. "Brother Dave, when God calls, we must be ready to preach, pray or die."

What choice did I have? God had called me and Brother Dan had invited me. The line between the two was erased with a nod of my head.

Three days later, I peered over the top of the oak pulpit for the first time as a preacher. Homework, trombone, and model airplanes had all been pushed aside for a pre-adolescent try at sermonizing. Little did I know it at the time, but I intuitively followed the advice given later in seminary by a homiletics professor:

> Read yourself full,
> Pray yourself hot,
> Preach yourself empty.

Isaiah's vision of the Lord in the sixth chapter of his prophecy became my text for two reasons. One was that the action-packed story had always fired my imagination. The other reason was equally simple. My father's five-volume library of religious books included a broken-down, mismatched commentary on the book of Isaiah. From that commentary, I pilfered the inevitable three-point outline:

1. Isaiah saw God

2 Isaiah saw himself

3. Isaiah saw his calling

Adapting bits and pieces of theological and literary phrases, including one essential reference to a word, ". . .as it is interpreted in Hebrew," I exercised my new-found skill at outlining that my eighth-grade teacher had drilled into us as preparation for high school. What I said in that first sermon is lost in the dead storage of "Worthwhile Things to Forget." How I said it lives on.

In true Tabernacle style, I slid over the glory of the shining God that Isaiah saw in favor of the fringe benefits of heaven—no sin, no tears, no sickness, no sorrow. Just the mention of heaven evoked shouts that marked the transition from my "firstly" to my "secondly."

Thirteen-year-olds know more about sin than about heaven. Isaiah's cry, "*Woe is me, for I am undone*" was ready-made for an eventual altar call. But all of my words and gestures were building toward a sure winner of the text when Isaiah reported:

"*An angel took a hot coal from off the altar and touched my lips.*" (Isa 6:6)

"FIRE" in any form ignited the Tabernacle-ites, so I pounded and stomped for an out-pouring of a red-hot revival in our midst. Like matches in a tinderbox, I struck every cliche about fire that I had collected from other preachers:

> "white hot for God"
> "on the firing line"
> "tongues of fire"
> "living fire"
> "purifying fire"

They worked—too well. "Aye-mens" and "Preach it, Brother Dave" echoed and re-echoed across the Tabernacle. Saints stood and shouted. Grandpa Mac did his jig in the aisle and Sister Ida Mae's tear-limp handkerchief signaled Holy Surrender. Together, they set in a motion the hypnotic beat of chorus after chorus of the old Gospel song,

> *"'Tis burning in my soul,*
> *'Tis burning in my soul,*
> *The fire of heavenly love*
> *Is burning in my soul."*

My first sermon peaked too soon. Tongue-tied and flat-footed, I just stood there. Moments before, I had been intoxicated by my power over people. Now, I was confused, frustrated and on the edge of panic. How do you preach a "thirdly" that is an anticlimax? Or, how do you close an aborted sermon?

A half-man, half-child handles this kind of situation with tears. Just as my eyes were beginning to fill and panic was grabbing at my throat, a firm hand gripped my shoulder from behind. Thank God, Brother Dan sensed my plight and took control. "God has spoken through Brother Dave. Let us pray."

Tagging on to my last words about "fire" Brother Dan prayed a scorching sermon upon sinners and a searing exhortation upon lukewarm saints. I slumped in fake prayer on the sacred sofa reserved for ministers of the Gospel, squinting through my fingers and hoping against hope that no one would come to the altar. I should not have feared. Only Brother Allen's eight-year-old daughter came forward, a precious child. She answered every altar call.

Then and there, I decided that preaching was hard business. Soul-winning sounded so easy when evangelists reported the results. For me, it turned out to be physically exhausting and ego-devastating. Was there any compensation? I counted on Grandpa McKenna for the answer.

Immediately after the benediction, I hurried down the pulpit steps toward Grandpa to get his appraisal. If he blessed me, I would preach forever; if he rejected me, I would go plant corn. Neither happened. When I edged up to him so close that his restricted vision and shortened memory would focus on me, I got the wrong answer. Like a doctor hedging on his diagnosis, Grandpa Mac said, "David, you might make a preacher yet."

I felt damned by the faintest praise. If only he had applauded me with one of his patented shouts, or less than that, if only he had anointed me with a touch of his hand, all of my pain would have disappeared. But, in listening for his words and longing for his hand, I missed the gleam in his clouded eyes. Later on, I found out that he was pumped with pride, but dared not show it. Wisdom told him that his grandson's promise for preaching was exceeded only by the size of his ego. He knew that something in me had to die before I could ever preach.

9

Where Is My Wandering Boy Tonight?

Sooty puffs of smoke from the departing train signaled my new-found freedom and symbolized my left-over taste for sin. Dad and Mom were heading for an anniversary weekend in Chicago, leaving me, a 16-year-old boy, with time, money, a driver's license and the family car. Already, a kaleidoscope of stored-up fantasies tumbled over and over in my mind as I mechanically waved "Goodbye" to the blurred images on the departing train. Waiting just long enough to be sure that my folks had lost their angle for looking back, I spun and sprinted off the platform toward my grey steed of potential wickedness—a 1938 Plymouth with a clean ashtray and an unsullied back seat. "Hey, what-a-ya-doing this weekend? My folks have gone and I've got the car."

I uttered the tingling words into the first telephone I found. Dick, my best non-Christian friend (coming from strong Lutheran family didn't count under the norms of the Tabernacle) by virtue of building model airplanes and playing brass instruments together, answered, "Great. How about a movie tomorrow night?"

"Gulp!" I expected smoking, drinking, dancing, necking—anything but a movie. Foolish or not, to me a movie had become the epitome of evil. Was it the cowardly fear of exposure in a public place or was it the connection that Brother Dan had drawn between sin and darkness in his preaching? As foolish as it seems, grosser sins had lesser fears for me.

Sin and movies became synonymous when my folks got religion. At one time, they fed me depression dimes for the Saturday matinees—Hop-Along Cassidy, Roy Rogers, Tom Mix, Tonto, Flash Gordon, and The Three Musketeers. One Saturday, the dimes stopped just after Flash Gordon's spaceship crashed. To this day, I do not know how the serial ended. If it hadn't been for my comic books, which survived my parents' purge of Saturday movies and Sunday newspapers, the likes of Flash Gordon would have been totally exterminated by the death-to-the-world ray that zapped me when my folks found God.

Sometime later, a sermon on "Hollywood, Harlots and Hell" sealed the transfer of my parents' new convictions to me. Brother Dan took as his double-barreled text, II Kings 9:30:

"And when Jehu was come to Jezreel, Jezebel heard of it; and she painted her face, and tied her hair, and looked out a window." To punctuate his point, the preacher jumped to II Kings 9:36:

". . .in the portion of Jezreel shall dogs eat the flesh of Jezebel." A simple sermonic syllogism followed:

> Major Premise: Jezebel was a harlot who painted her face
>
> Minor Premise: All Hollywood actresses paint their faces
>
> Conclusion: All Hollywood actresses are harlots.

Point by point, the case was made. Jezebel's blood-red lips and cheeks were to be matched by the gore from her crushed body when she was thrown from an upper window. God had spoken in His wrath—not only against spiritual harlots who sold their souls to the devil, but against anyone who painted their lips or followed the movie stars. On the Etch-a-Sketch of my impressionable mind, a movie theater that had once been an Eden of my innocence was now the sign and seal of my damnation.

Should I or shouldn't I go to a movie with Dick? Faust-like, I traced three circles on the floor of the telephone booth before screwing up the courage to chirp, "Sure, I'll pick you up."

Light years of conscience later, I took my first step through the flaming swords that divided the bright foyer of the theater from the inner darkness. Squinting and ducking until my pupils adjusted to the sight of sin, I slouched into a seat, envying the boldness of my buddy. My memory of skipping school to see Laurel and Hardy haunted me. But this time, the movie started and my fears dissolved.

According to contemporary ratings, the musical comedy that we saw would be rated a double "G." To my surprise, Jezebels with angelic faces and divine legs sang and danced as if they were really happy. Periodically, I looked up to see if the roof was cracking or wondered if God would entertain a contradictory headline, "David McKenna Raptured from a Movie Theater." Soon these thoughts passed and I became fully absorbed in the romance on the silver screen.

"THE END" came too quickly. Only one obstacle remained to complete my sinful coup. Could I escape without being seen? Fleeting comfort came when I thought, "If I see any other Christians leaving the theater, they'll be guilty too." Then, I reasoned, "What if they are on the other side of the street when we walk out? Or what if they're stopped in a car at the red light on the corner?" Whatever the odds were, I took no chance. Slinking under the armpit of my taller buddy, I hurried him to the shadows and the relief of outer darkness.

After cruising "The Ave" in American Graffiti style we stopped at a grocery store to call and ask if Dick could spend the night with me. Dick posed the question and then stopped to listen before turning back to me to say, "Your dad called. They came home early and wanted you to know."

Not without a flashback of Jezebel's bloody body, my quivering question was, "What did your dad say?"

"He told your dad that we were at a movie."

"Confound these Lutherans," I thought, "They drink, smoke, go to shows and still claim to be Christians." Why didn't Dick's dad keep his mouth shut? Prison doors slammed and manacles snapped on my short-lived freedom. Dropping off my buddy, who was still trying to figure out why a Saturday night show created a family crisis, I pointed the bow of the three-masted schooner on the hood of the Plymouth toward home, sailing into the teeth of the wind and toward the eye of the storm.

God is full of surprises! By the time I arrived home, Dad and Mom were in bed, exhausted from their quick turnaround trip. There was no cross-examination or hint of distrust. Dad explained that Chicago had lost its glamour for them now that they were Christians and Mom simply groaned in her sleep. Relieved of my worst fears, I relaxed in the rationalization that I had not done anything wrong. After all, the movie was good, God didn't kill me, and my folks didn't care. Guiltless sleep came quickly.

But, why sin if you can't talk about it? Between Sunday school and church the next morning, I broke out of my preacher-to-be image by bragging to my buddies, "Have you seen the new show at the State Theatre?" For the first time, I puffed at my one-upmanship with the hardcore, teenage sinners who could put on great stone faces as their mothers wept,

"Where is my wandering boy tonight?
The boy of my tend'rest care;
The boy that was once my joy and light,
The child of my love and prayer?"

To cap my triumph, Brother Dan's sermon did not give the slightest hint that God had whispered my name to him. For once, neither worldliness nor backsliding served as the penetration point for his thunderbolts. Confirmed by the silence of God, I walked out of church making plans for my next movie.

Usually, Sunday dinner was a family affair. To compensate for the taboo against fun and games, we ate a hefty meal and then my sister and I settled down into The Bobbsey Twins or Tom Swift while waiting for Mother and Dad to finish their "always on

Sunday" nap routine. But more often than not, we traded invitations with other families of the Tabernacle. This Sunday was no exception. We were to be dinner guests of a couple who lived on a farm three or four miles outside of town. I was anxious to go because she was a good cook and he had a collection of antique guns that fascinated me. So, wafting on a seventh-heaven cloud, I chattered like a jaybird with my friends after church while waiting for my parents.

How far the mighty fall! Dad came to me to say, "Son, I have to drop by the house before going out to the Curtises'. Mother and Pat are going to ride with them. Would you like to go with me?"

"Sure." Dad was my ideal and every moment alone with him was a special privilege.

Dad didn't take the direct route. First, he stopped at the house for a camera. Then, he headed toward the back roads that doubled the miles to the Curtis home. The camera and the countryside made sense. When Dad gave up sailing because of the Tabernacle taboo on Sunday sports, he switched his hobby to photography. On this occasion, my role was clear to me. Relaxing in the passenger's seat, I became Dad's partner in a visual search for a subject along the roadside that met the requirements for figure and ground, light and shadow, range of focus, and depth of field. Artistic agreement contracted silence between us.

By now, every guard was down. As long as I live, I will always feel the shock of the words that Dad spoke out of silence: "Did you enjoy the movie last night?" Waves of disbelief stunned me. My Dad had trapped me! My tongue was turned to stone. "Did you enjoy the movie last night?" Dad repeated his matter-of-fact inquiry.

Slowly, my sense of guilt and betrayal took verbal form, not in confession, but in belligerence. "Yes, I did." I answered with honest defiance.

Dad resisted the temptation to counterattack with equal hostility. Instead, he set up another decoy with the same even level of questioning, "What was the movie about?"

Assuming that I had won the offensive again, I went into an animated review of the romantic script and the dazzling performance of the stars.

Dad listened without interruption until I finished. Silence again. I basked in the obvious triumph of my eloquent defense . . . that is, until Dad pronounced his verdict in the same tone with which he had asked the first question, "Son, If you choose to go to movies, don't use my money or drive my car."

He cut my heart out. I wanted to scream, "Beat me, ground me, consign me to Hell . . . but don't ask me to feel as if I disappointed you."

Nothing more was ever said. My conscience bore the stripes of a lashing that could never be matched by an inquisitor's whip or a preacher's tongue. Dad was the god of my life and hell was his disappointment.

Years went by before I risked a movie again. Even then, I rationalized my re-entry by choosing a Cinerama travelogue. With that success under my belt, I next opted for a biblical spectacular based on a legend and embellished by just enough sex and violence to be a box office hit. Upon leaving the theater I commented to friends, "You know, a story like that means so much more if you are already a Christian."

Defense mechanisms are no longer needed to justify my attendance at theaters. Have I gained or lost? Is it better to be free from blushing in shame when yesterday's sin is today's standard? Or, is it better to have a conscience beaten raw by the fear of disappointing a beloved parental model?

Someplace in between, there is a freedom of discipline that dispels the shadow on my shoulder put there by Mother's frequent warning, "Be sure your sin will find you out."

10

Bringing In the Sheaves

MOTHER OPENED FAMILY DEVOTIONS with the tone of a military general briefing the troops for battle. "Cousin Dolly is coming to visit us next week. She needs to get away from home because her father is drunk almost all of the time. Also, her mother tells me that the neighborhood where they live is fast becoming a real slum. It won't be easy because Dolly is a Catholic. Let's pray for her tonight."

Three days later, Cousin Dolly appeared at the front door, suitcase in hand. Peering into the crack of daylight between Mother's body and the doorframe, I saw the grown-up version of a former childhood playmate. The vision in the doorway demanded a double-take. Blue mascara romanticized her Latin eyes, deep red color projected her lips into lush prominence, and a shorts and halter outfit strategically covered the shapely surprise of well-distributed baby-fat.

After the startle effect wore off, Mother kissed and hugged Cousin Dolly into our household. I chose to shake hands for fear of touching the wrong place in a hug or betraying the awakened impulses of my adolescence in a kiss. Mother had always said that girls are at least two years physically older than boys. Dolly proved it. I was 15; she was 16 going on 21.

One condition accompanied Cousin Dolly's visit. All of the religious rituals of our fundamentalist home had to be observed—Protestant grace at the dinner table, evening Scripture and prayers at the family altar, and an empty house during Sunday worship, Tuesday Missionary Circle, Wednesday prayer meeting, and Friday evangelistic hour. Nothing, not even a mission of mercy, could interfere with our family's quest for holiness.

If Cousin Dolly wished, transportation was provided for her to go to Confession and Mass, but only if scheduled around our attendance at the "True" Means of Grace.

Despite the blunt admonitions of her mother and the subtle preachments of our household, Cousin Dolly remained a free spirit. After grace at meals, she would cross herself and say, "That takes care of that." And on Friday, she nibbled on the meat after finishing the fish that my mother had prepared especially for her. "Oh, well," she shrugged, "I have to go to Confession next week, and anyway, I'm not sure that I'll ever get out of Purgatory now."

Secretly, I admired her, but publicly I would have been quick to confirm that her slapstick remarks verified all of the evils of Roman Catholicism against which Brother Dan preached so vehemently:

"The Pope is the Anti-Christ;

"Rome is not the Holy City—it is the seat of Hell!

"Priests who mumble in Latin and smoke black cigars are tools of the Devil;

"Catholics who sin and confess, sin and confess, sin and confess are lost in the darkness of night."

According to these indictments, Cousin Dolly deserved pity and prayer. Occasionally, I would hear my mother telling her, "Dolly, the Catholic Church cannot save you. Only Jesus can."

Always in good humor, Cousin Dolly laughed, "But, Aunt Helen, I do believe in Jesus."

Try as she might, mother never seemed to prove her assumption that Cousin Dolly suffered as a starving, sinful soul who was hungry to repent at the mention of Jesus' name. Reluctantly, she quit preaching, but never failed to mention her unsaved niece in her evening prayers.

Each time our pre-church routine began, mother invited Dolly to come along. Each time, she answered, "Oh, no, the priest would excommunicate me and my mother would kill me." Cousin Dolly relied on that stock answer three or four times until either mother's prayers or her curiosity got the best of her. One Sunday evening, without advance notice, Dolly appeared in the dining room ready for church, or more appropriately, Confession. Blue eyelids flirted upward to display the impish anticipation in her dark eyes, "I'd like to go to your church tonight. How do I look?"

A fashion model's spin on spiked heels lifted the black silk dress into a ballet dancer's flare, revealing seamless, black-netted stockings, and almost sending her veiled, matching pillbox hat into orbit. Of course, I thought, a Roman Catholic woman always covers her head in church, but do they always wear so much junk—dangling earbobs, a flashing bodice pin, and rings on both hands? What would the plain sisters in orthopedic shoes and shapeless dresses think? Instinctively, I knew what mother thought: "Cousin Dolly just hasn't had the light."

Off we went with another trophy of mother's prayers. On the way, she began to hum the Gospel song that everyone in the car knew, except Cousin Dolly:

> *"Bringing in the sheaves,*
> *Bringing in the sheaves,*
> *We shall come rejoicing,*
> *Bringing in the sheaves."*

Unless you are part of the evangelistic tradition, you cannot fully appreciate what it means to bring a stranger, a sinner, and a Roman Catholic to an old-fashioned revival meeting. At The Evangelistic Mission Tabernacle, such a person was a "Happening." Otherwise, the hellfire and damnation sermons were just reruns for the lukewarm, the backslidden, and the neurotic. So, our family's processional up the stairs and into the sanctuary had the bearing of a triumphal entry. In keeping with the motto on the bulletin board, "You are only a stranger once," official ushers and volunteer greeters met us at the back of the church to hear my mother announce, "This is my niece, Dolly. She's from Detroit and is staying with us for a few days."

Whatever esoteric signal passed through those words, Cousin Dolly heard a mixture of Southern drawls, Michigan nasals, and Hoosier slurs recite: "Pleased to meetcha," "Gawd bless you," and "Glad to have you all here." Not one pharisaical look of condemnation or condescension spoiled the introductions.

Hospitality ruled over sanctity until Brother Dan's grand entrance. Exiting from the pre-service prayer room at the back of the church, God's Man of the Hour displayed the symbols of Shekinah Glory—eyes that simultaneously revealed the puff of a tearful burden along with the gleam of a visitation within the Veil. To this aura, Brother Dan added his symbolic gesture of authority to preach the Gospel. His right hand enfolded the Holy Bible high against his chest, another badge of spiritual distinction. When I started carrying my Bible to church, guess where I held it?

Brother Dan's entrance cued the congregation to be seated. Voices slid into whispers and everyone filed down the aisles to their seats. The more devout knelt and groaned one final prayer for the service. With his own sense of appropriate timing and low-key pageantry, Brother Dan stepped into his one-man processional down the side aisle. On this occasion, he interrupted his march to the pulpit by stopping at the row where Dad, Mom, Sister Pat, and Cousin Dolly were seated. Genuine warmth flowed through his welcome to the only stranger in our midst.

On to the pulpit. Brother Dan's ritual always included a direct line to the divan for dignitaries behind the pulpit. There, he bowed on one knee, Bible now shifted to his left breast, and right hand cupping his forehead. A holy, expectant hush settled upon the congregation as all eyes fixed upon the reverent figure in black whose only pride was betrayed by the slick, black hair that glistened under the lights.

Brother Dan had gone down slowly, but when the silence confirmed his full control, he sprang to his feet, swept his trombone off the stand, and tongued a musical note for the evening service:

> *"When we all get to heaven,*
> *What a day of rejoicing that will be;*
> *When we all see Jesus,*
> *We'll sing and shout the victory."*

Bounding from orchestra to pulpit during the last notes of the chorus, Brother Dan waved the congregation to its feet with the jubilant call: "Well, bless God. If you've got a little bit of heaven in your soul tonight, sing with me, '*When We All Get to Heaven* . . .'"

Experience told me that there would be a hot time in the old Tabernacle tonight. "Sing it again. Let the devil know we're here. If you've got the victory tonight, wave your hand as we repeat the chorus. Hey, the Psalmist told us to praise God on ten-stringed instruments. Do you know what he meant? He meant your hands . . . ten fingers clapping to the beat of the hymn. Some of you need to loosen up your ten-stringed instruments and praise the Lord. Clap your hands as we sing the chorus once again. This time, when we come to the last stanza and are singing, 'When we all see Jesus' let's hold the 'all' and see who can hold it the longest—the orchestra, the choir or the congregation. Ready now? Watch me . . . "

With a little cheating, the orchestra won and the red-faced Buddha of a clarinetist almost turned blue with bloat before he fell off the high "C" into an anticlimactic squeak.

> "AAAAAAAAAAAAAAAA. . . .LLLLLLLLLLLL. . .
> SEE. . .
> . . .JESUS,
> We'll sing and SHOUT the victory!"
> "Well, Praise the Lord."

Brother Dan knew how to handle emotional peaks. "As soon as you are seated, I want five people to stand back up and give a victory report. Who'll be first? Sister Ida Mae? Sister Dorothy?

Brother Paul? Brother Jim? WAIT! I asked for five and already there are eight on their feet. THE LORD IS HERE. Sister Ida Mae, you were first."

As the drama escalated, Cousin Dolly's twisting and turning disclosed her fascination with the greatest religious show on earth. Whether it was fear at the frolic of Protestant worship or curiosity with the unknown tongue of our spiritualized language, she kept nudging my mother and quizzing, "What's he doing now?" or "What did she mean by that?"

Sister Ida Mae's testimony thoroughly mystified her: "Even after I was saved, I had carnality in my heart. The Old Man in me was at war with the New Man. But, last Friday night, I prayed clear through to victory. Tonight, Hallelujah, The Old Man's dead and The New Man is filled with the Holy Spirit."

Mother could only answer, "Shhhh" and promise, "I'll tell you later."

Relief came during a vocal solo when the "Aye-mens" were largely confined to the corner reserved for their utterance. Prayer followed. To refute the proud and stiff-necked Methodists who stood for prayer, we always knelt. Little did we know that the Methodists' loss was the Roman Catholics' gain. For the first time that evening, Cousin Dolly knew what to do. She genuflected toward an imaginary high altar, crossed herself and created Hands of Prayer while kneeling straight up over the seat in front of her. She was alone because Tabernacle-ites turned and buried their heads against the backrest of their theater seats. Sometime later, I heard about a new convert who mused, "Why do we put our head where our bottom was when we talk to God?"

Dad, who had been asked to lead in prayer, was the exception. On one knee in the aisle, his head pointed up and he saluted God loudly and clearly,

> "OUR FATHER . . . (groundswell of "Aye-mens")
> WE COME TO YOU TONIGHT . . ("Yes, Yes, Lord")
> TO ASK YOUR BLESSING UPON THIS SERVICE . . .
> ("Make it so, Lord")

HEAR US AS WE PRAY . . . ("Aye-men, Aye-men, Aye-men")

Competitive prayers broke upward in a cacophony of sound. Dad's intonements grew and grew in volume until his voice merged into the high-pitched drone of a hundred petitioners bombarding the Throne of Grace. Before the last "Aye-men," weeping voices could be heard tracking down wandering sons and wayward daughters, calling down judgment on our wicked city, and penetrating into remote heathen villages until the whole world was wrapped in the cocoon of all-encompassing prayer.

Dad's final "Aye-men" was equally contagious. Rippling across the headless pews, antiphonal "Aye-mens" pitched and rolled in a lowering tide. Soon, amidst the shuffle of rising, there was only a groan or two, either the leftover of fervent prayer or the carryover of extra weight.

Necessary evils came next—announcements. "Tuesday morning at 10 a.m. will be special request time in prayer. Whatever your need may be, bring it to the altar of God. If you are not working, you should be here. Wednesday night is prayer meeting, the mid-week feast for your soul. Thursday is Work Night here at the church. We need 50 people to help revarnish the back pews. God's house must be our first thought . . . "

(My first thought was the dilapidated trailers and temporary government housing in which so many of the transplants among us lived.)

"Be in much prayer for the Friday night Evangelistic Hour. Reverend Jimmy Miller, an internationally known evangelist and soul winner will be here. If you are really concerned about souls, you will come early for the seven o'clock revival prayer-time and you will bring an unsaved friend with you . . . "

Cousin Dolly?

"Then, with our August camp-meeting just two weeks away, I am calling for a night of prayer around the altar after the service. Revival must begin with us. Lost souls will never be won as long as there is ease in Zion. Eight hours of sleep is nothing compared to an eternity in Hell for your friends and loved ones if you let them down. Of course, next Sunday will have our regular order of services. Every time the door of this church opens, a little bell should be ringing in your heart."

Another moment of reprieve was granted as a last-minute, put-together trio searched for the notes and the harmony of the old West Virginia gospel song, "Life Is Like a Mountain Railroad." Behind them on the pastoral couch, Brother Dan nervously flipped back and forth through his Bible, spread-eagled his fingers over a bowed forehead, and occasionally encouraged the struggling sirens with a bright "Aye-men."

I should explain that the pronouncement of "Amen" served as another telltale spiritual sign. When the zeal of the Lord was lost, "Ah-men" was the formal perversion of the old-fashioned "Aye-men". Our church held that Episcopalian priests with starchy, white, backward collars use "Ah-men" to seal their semi-pagan liturgy, and that Presbyterians nailed their spiritual coffins shut with the organ dirge "Ahhh—hh—men" at the end of their apparently lifeless chants.

So, to a chorus of "Aye-mens" the trio concluded its musical mis-production. Brother Dan flushed out one more covey of rushing sound when he reminded his people that trained voices and good music were not substitutes for the melody of the Holy Spirit. He went on in transition: "After all, these services belong to God. We may plan them, but He can rule and overrule at any time. Moments ago, for instance, while I was seeking the mind of God for the message of the evening, He changed my text and my subject. Thank God, because the Truth never cools off. I'll preach on the announced text next Sunday."

Everyone moved forward to the edge of their seats. A Spirit-interrupted sermon was second only to a Spirit-interrupted service. "If you have your Bibles, turn with me to the Book of Romans, the twelfth chapter and the second verse . . . (pages flutter). '*BE NOT CONFORMED TO THIS WORLD; BUT BE YE TRANSFORMED BY THE RENEWING OF YOUR MIND.*'"

As if to establish divine authority for every pronouncement that would follow, Brother Dan emphatically read the text again and asked the people to keep their Bibles open to the passage while he preached. Unless something unusual happened, this would be the last reference to the text or its context. Bibles were primarily tokens of sanctity enfolded for the world to see on the Via Dolorosa between the parking lot and the front door of the church. Once inside, the same Bible was transposed into a baton for the sovereign Word as it was passed from God to Brother Dan in a perfect handoff.

"We are a nation at war. Many of our young men-ah are on some battlefield right now-ah giving their lives for our freedom. They know what it means to take orders. When General Eisenhower sent out the command to attack the Normandy Beach, the order went down the line-ah to the lowliest private—ATTACK AT DAWN! When the general commands-ah, everyone obeys-ah.

"God is the supreme commander of the Christian army. He also gives the orders. Here is one, ' . . . Be not conformed to this world.' God first gave this order to the Apostles who lived in the first century. They obeyed and died. And to every generation since that time-ah, God has had an army of His people who will obey His orders and not be conformed to this world-ah.

"Today is no different. God, our Commander, has ordered us-ah to separate ourselves from the world-ah whether you are a captain-ah or just a private-ah on the battlefield for your Lord."

"OH, GLORY, GLORY, GLORY" Sister Haley, abandoned by an alcoholic husband and left on welfare with five ungrateful and delinquent kids, had seen a light at the end of her dark tunnel. Preacher and people waited patiently while she waltzed in the aisle, hanky afloat, and tears fanning out through the washes of wrinkles around her eyes. No one would deny her a moment of hope.

Brother Dan saw his opening, "Do you know why Sister Haley has the victory tonight? Look at her. You don't see her-ah wearing sleeveless dresses or prancing with frizzy hair cut in a beauty parlor. Even the name is a lie. If you want to go to a real beauty parlor, come to this altar at the front of the church-ah, repent of your sins-ah, and let God put the Beauty of Holiness on your face.

You won't need the fashions and fad of this world-ah if God gives you his beauty treatment."

("Preach it, brother, preach it.")

Energized by "Aye-men Harry," the toothless and sexless survivor of three divorces and two common-law wives, the fiery-eyed preacher hit a fever pitch.

"Listen, once you cut the sleeves out of your dresses-ah, you soon cut your hair-ah. That's the way the devil operates. Soon he'll have you looking just like the world. Your eyes will look like you dunked your head in an ashcan. Your lips and your fingernails will look like you have been squashing bed-bugs all night-ah. And then-ah, you know what happens? YOU BEGIN TO PUT ON JUNK-AH! Gold, pearls and costly array . . . like earbobs that hang down and dangle."

Embarrassed silence took over the congregation. Brother Dan had stepped across the Maginot Line between preaching and meddling. Even though the women of the Tabernacle could not afford the accoutrements of fashion, they may have nursed a secret desire for a pearl or two. Or, perhaps there was an unconscious sense of protocol that Brother Dan had violated with a sleeveless, bobbed, painted and bedecked stranger in their midst.

Provoked by the silence, the preacher jumped from behind the pulpit to the opening in the vanity curtain and stabbed out in anger, "Do you know what dangling earbobs are? They are stirrups where the Devil puts his feet when he rides your soul!"

A laugh, a pause, and then a shock of innocence. In full voice, Cousin Dolly said, "OH, MY GAWD, HE'S TALKING ABOUT ME!!" Cousin Dolly reached up and plucked the accursed stirrups from her ears. Heads turned on swivels to stare at the source of the sound.

"Swallow me, earth," I wished without words. Awkwardness prevailed for all of us and I can remember my hostile thought, "If I were Dolly, I would walk out."

Instead, we just sat there, victims of a concocted, one-point sermon that scored and left us numb. Whatever else happened in that service is lost to memory. If Brother Dan worked his usual strategy, he retreated into innocuous ramblings that led to an altar call with a few impressionable souls responding. Cousin Dolly stood strong through the repeated pleadings of the invitational hymn. Secretly, I admired the strength of her resistance.

Our family had entered the church in triumph; we left in defeat. Somehow, Cousin Dolly's worldliness had contaminated us among the church people and erected a non-verbal barrier between us at home. Religion was no longer a subject in our strained conversation.

To this day, I don't know what happened after church that night. In any case, Cousin Dolly's vacation was cut short when her brother appeared at the door the next morning to take her home.

Thirty years elapsed before I heard from Cousin Dolly again. Only the information about her marriage to a man named Fred and the birth of five children had been squeezed through the family grapevine.

It came in the mail. The name on the envelope was not even familiar to me. Inside, as best I remember, the letter read:

> Dear Cousin Dave:
>
> I am married to your Cousin Dolly. Even though we have never met, I had to write and tell you the good news. Last Sunday evening in our home, Dolly and I met the Lord Jesus Christ. He was introduced to us by our son, John. After he returned from some rough years in the service, he became connected with the Coral Ridge Presbyterian Church where the Bible is preached and people are saved.
>
> John's life was a mess until he met Jesus. Dolly and I couldn't understand the peace and joy that John had until he invited the minister to come and explain it to us. We, too, were empty and lost. When the pastor told us the simple story of Jesus, we knew that we had found the answer. In our living room, Dolly and I knelt and asked Jesus to forgive us our sins and live in us.
>
> How I wish that I could explain the difference that the Lord has made in our home. Every day is filled with love and we have seen all of our children saved one by one. Jesus worked another miracle when I asked our

> pastor if he knew you. He said, "Of course I do, let me give you his address." I had to write to tell you what Christ has done for us. We are now serving him by hosting a radio program of religious music associated with our church. Dolly has mentioned your mother from time to time and said, "I wish that Aunt Helen were alive to know that her prayers are finally answered."
>
> Love, in Christ
> Fred and Dolly

I weep as I write. God's ways are not our ways. Who am I to say that Cousin Dolly's anguished cry was not the awakening call for her salvation?

"O, MY GAWD, HE'S TALKING ABOUT ME!!"

11

Oh, Why Not Tonight?

"MOM! DAD!" MY CASUAL call reverberated through the house without an answer.

"Mo-o-m!! DAD!!" My yell was swallowed in the mouth of the chambered staircase.

What's wrong? My folks had driven directly home from the Sunday evening evangelistic meeting at the Tabernacle. They should be here!

I had walked home, taking the circuitous route uptown and past Ceccarilli's Ice Cream Parlor, the high school hangout. My sin was to escape the wrenching conviction that had been laid upon my soul by Brother Dan's sermon on the Second Coming of Christ. One measure of relief was to go to the altar—again. Instead, I rationalized that my sins were only wishes. So, when the final benediction lifted the pressure to repent, I opted to walk off the remains of conviction rather than ride home with the family.

Three circles around the block brought me past Ceccarelli's for the third time. My sinful wish was that the worldly girl whom I secretly loved would come out the door and say "Hello" to me. What a fantasy! I didn't know if she was inside.

Still, I sauntered past the place that Brother Dan had labeled a "den of wickedness." Never, never, never would I voluntarily enter an ice cream parlor on a Sabbath evening. My 16-year-old soul was still tight in the vice of that sermon on the Second Coming. What if Christ should come while I was in that place? Even though I had not responded to the invitation to repent, I had no intention of letting a 10-cent Coke further reduce my chances of being caught up to meet Him in the clouds.

"MOTHER!! DAD!! ARE YOU HERE?"

Subterranean guilt flooded to the surface and joined the haunt of an empty home. I was alone and my parents were gone. But where?

Brother Dan's text from Matthew 14:41–42 was rerun in technicolor before my eyes,

> *There shall two be in the field; the one shall be taken,*
> *And the other left. Two women shall be grinding at the mill;*
> *The one shall be taken, and the other left.*
> *Watch therefore: for ye know not what hour your Lord shall come.*

Of course, Brother Dan updated and embellished the Word of God. "When Christ returns to catch His Bride, a train will be speeding down the track—the engineer is ready to meet His Lord, the fireman is not. I see a flash of light, but not a sound. The fireman turns around to find the engineer missing. Frantically, he looks around, out, up, and then down—the only trace is a pile of clothes in the corner of the cab—blue-striped coveralls, gray engineer's cap, and a red bandanna!" Dropping his voice to a wistful hush, God's man intoned, "What a sad sight it will be in some of the homes of people who are here tonight. A mother is taken, a father is left. Little sister is gone, big brother remains. O sinner, won't you get ready to meet your Lord? Jesus may come before this night is out."

Six verses and nine refrains of "Oh, Why Not Tonight?" followed. Needless to say, a 16-year-old with secret thoughts and sinful wishes would be condemned by the dreadful dirge,

> *"Tomorrow's sun may never rise*

To bless thy long deluded sight;
This is the time, Oh, then, be wise,
Be saved, O tonight.
Oh, why not tonight? Oh, why not tonight?
Wilt thou be saved? Then why not tonight?"

A stumble onto the landing of the second floor of our home jolted me back to reality. Frenzy took over where fear left off. After two swipes at the light switch in the master bedroom, the light came on and I looked—not for parents, but for two piles of clothes—Mother's dark blue dress with the Puritan collar and Dad's grey stripe suit with dromedary bumps raised by the shoes underneath.

Not a trace. Room to room, I raced—upstairs, downstairs, searching for the telltale signs of my raptured family. Then I remembered, Brother Dan predicted splitting skies and a blinding light through which the Son of God would appear in all His glory.

Ripping back the bedroom curtains, a flash of light startled me sightless.

HE HAS COME!

Or has He? Would Christ return to earth in an automobile? Two headlights had turned into our driveway.

THEY HAVE COME!

My parents were home. God in His great mercy had spared me once again. Before I slept that night, I knelt beside my bed to pay the premium on both Fire and Flight Insurance by asking God to forgive my sinful wishes.

Strange, but sermons on the Second Coming scared me more than hellfire and brimstone. If I had been in the congregation when Jonathan Edwards preached his Puritan classic, "Sinners in the Hands of an Angry God," I would have joined the conscience-stricken crowd who took a white-knuckle grip on the pew to keep from sliding into Hell. Not being present at that sermon, I would rank "Prophecy from the Pyramids" as the all-time mover and shaker for me.

Scientific sophistication was the strategy of the nationally advertised evangelist who presented "Prophecy from the Pyramids."

Playing deftly upon the title of "Doctor" that preceded his name on advertisements, the evangelist lectured from giant, multi-colored charts. Each graphic showcard highlighted cutaways of The Great Pyramid in Egypt. The Doctor authoritatively guided his pointer like a scepter from one chart to another. Soon, the magic of prophetic translation wafted through to us. Corridors, passageways, vaults and antechambers portrayed the times and events of human history. The portal to The Great Pyramid signified Creation. Immediately thereafter, a tunneled corridor dropped a hazardous step like the Fall of Man. Down, down, down the tunnel slid until it bottomed out in a pit that might have been Hell itself. Only the mercy of a loving God permitted a temporary escape upward through the maze of Hebrew history. After a torturous climb, the tunnel burst open into a magnificent antechamber that held the treasure of the king—spiritually, nothing less than the Advent of Jesus Christ Himself.

Back into the tunnel again. Man now inched his way down through the Dark Ages, up through the breathing room of the Reformation, and down again though the deceptive opening of the Renaissance. The Doctor's pointer came to rest on the narrowest stricture of all—the 20th century. Mankind is forced to its belly and must crawl serpent-like through the tight sphincters of world wars and moral corruption. History has spoken in judgment. If Christ delays His Coming, man will suffocate in the cul-de-sac of his sins. The tunnel appears to end with no more room for humanity to survive.

Head drooping, shoulders slumping, the Doctor dramatized every man's despair. Wait! A dip of the cloth, a brush of the hand. VOILA! Before our eyes, the heart of The Great Pyramid spatially exploded into the golden vault of Pharoah—God's glorious symbol for the Second Coming of Jesus Christ. Magic ink has mothered a miracle.

Momentarily, the Doctor slipped out of his role to lead his class in a dissonant version of the "Hallelujah Chorus." Before the last "Aye-men" is sounded, the conductor cut off the celebration with a down-and-out snap of the hand.

Doctor qua Evangelist turned Doctor again. He traded his pointer for a calibrated measuring scale. Placing it on the passageways of the master chart, the Doctor factually reported the findings of his research: "A scientific measurement of the length of the tunnel of the 20th century, in comparison with the known time of the other historical passages, reveals the exact year, month and day of the Rapture." Era by era, year by year, the Doctor marches time to its denouement: "JESUS WILL COME AGAIN ON APRIL 23, 1947!!" Brains spun and fingers counted. April 23, 1947 was just three months and thirteen days away!

The Doctor slid laterally into the role of a low-key Evangelist. "Do you know that The Chicago Tribune has already cast this headline in type, 'EXTRA, EXTRA, EXTRA. JESUS RETURNS'? Dear soul, are you ready?"

Sinners spewed from the pews to crowd out the long, long altar. Coming late, I had to repent on the tweedy cushion of a "Born Again" theater seat. Later that night, I prayed at my bedside, "Lord, I am now ready for your return, but will you hold your coming until I graduate from high school?"

Either the prophetic Doctor was wrong or a patient God answered my prayer. April 23, 1947 came and went. In more cynical moments, I have often wondered, "Did the Doctor of The Great Pyramid have a private rapture? Or, did he just change the date and take his charts into new territory?" Whatever the case, he never came through our parts again.

Despite the exposure of a false prophet, sermons on the Second Coming continued to haunt me. Relief came not from a preacher, but a poet. In high school, a teacher of literature required us to read John Greenleaf Whittier's "Abraham Davenport." Whittier was responding in verse to the mysterious Day of Darkness that blacked out New England on May 19, 1780.

Oh, how I identified with the men who prayed and the women who wept as they listened for the "doom blast of the trumpet" and looked for the "dreadful face of Christ." How I wanted to second the motion of the lawgivers in the old State House of Connecticut who trembled and proposed, "It is the Lord's Great Day! Let us adjourn."

A dead pause. Then I, with the lawgivers, turned to hear the solitary figure who stood to speak against the motion. Abraham Davenport cleaved the intolerable hush with a steady voice,

"This may well be
The Day of Judgment which the world awaits;
But be it so or not, I only know
My present duty, and my Lord's command;
To occupy till He comes. So, at the post
Where He hath set me in His providence,
I choose, for one, to meet Him face to face;
No faithless servant frightened from my task,
But ready when the Lord of Harvest calls.
And therefore, with all reverence, I would say,
'Let God do His work, we will see to ours,
Bring in the candles.'"

Then, straight to the Order of the Day and with a dry natural sense of humor, Abraham Davenport debated an amendment to an act regulating shad and ale-wife fisheries:

. . . And there he stands in memory to this day,
Erect, self-poised, a rugged face, half seen
Against the background of unnatural dark,
A witness to the ages as they pass,
That simple duty hath no place for fear.

Never again would sermons on the Second Coming fill me with fear. Let the Rapture come! No screams, no tears for me. I'll be found doing something as simple as defending the rights of some poor fish.

12

The Cleansing Stream

FORTY FEET OF SOLID oak curling across the front of The Evangelistic Mission Tabernacle served as our mourner's bench. Second only to the power of the pulpit, the long, long altar marked the holy place for repentant sinners, backslidden saints, unsanctified believers, and fervent intercessors. Only the sight and smell of sawdust was missing.

Early in the unwritten catechism for the young of the Tabernacle was the dogma that everyone had to identify a time and place for being "born again." No room was allowed for Christians who grew gradually into grace or for those who could not remember when they made a U-turn into the narrow way. Spiritual credibility jumped notches when a believer testified to a 9:58 p.m. conversion at a tear-stained spot three and one-half feet from the north end of the long, long altar. Records in family Bibles were written to read:

> BORN: 9:03 a.m. August 23, 1920
> St. Luke's Hospital
> BORN AGAIN: 9:38 p.m. February 1, 1943
> The Evangelistic Mission Tabernacle

I was "born again" with two congenital defects. One was my conversion in a young people's testimony meeting where the full dramatic effect of a weeping and wailing sinner being transformed into a shouting and running saint was missing. The other was a deficiency of location. Splintery planks of a sawhorse altar gave me no place to point when I testified upstairs.

The remedy was an instantaneous, on-the-spot, Second Work of Grace called Sanctification. Confused by the sin that remained in my life after conversion, I was taught to seek perfection. Scriptural admonitions for sanctification were clear. God has spoken plainly in Hebrews 12:14:

> *"Follow peace with all men, and holiness,*
> *without which no man shall see the Lord."*

Jesus promised His disciples the Holy Spirit as their Comforter after His departure and ordered them to wait at Jerusalem until they were:

> *". . .endued with power from on high."*

At Pentecost, the Holy Spirit made His debut in a setting of:

> *". . .flaming tongues and rushing winds."*

Disciples who were 98-pound weaklings were transformed into muscular, miracle-working Atlases. Thus, from that time on, the Apostles posed a standard question to new converts,

> *"Have you received the Holy Ghost since you believed?"*

Any resemblance, however, between the Biblical revelation and the Tabernacle interpretation of sanctification was purely coincidental. My introduction to the doctrine of holiness came with an itinerant evangelist's illustration of sanctification as "dekittenizing the well." Proudly identifying himself as an ignorant, shoeless, ridge-running hillbilly, he promptly proved his point. Tossing rocks at the glass house of theological sophistication, he proceeded to clarify the confusing doctrine of Entire Sanctification (or, as he described the experience, "The Second Work of Grace). He began: "On our scrub farms in old Kentucky, we always had more cats than we could count. Now, you all know that cats have kittens."

A sly smile widened his lips and raised one eyebrow as he crossed into forbidden territory, " . . . and when you have more cats and kittens than you have rats and mice, you-all have to do something to give the rats a fightin' chance." (Ghoulish chuckle) "Daddy took care of that by throwing the extra kittens down the well and feeshing out their lil-ole carcasses with the bucket. But, one time, Daddy forgot to count the kittens he threw down the well. A few days later, our drinkin' water went bad.. Quick as a hummin' bird, Daddy say, 'Ah got to de-kittenize the well.' So, back he went with his bucket and feeshed and feeshed until he got all of the rottin' kitten out of there. Right away, our drinkin'water cleared up and became pure again.

"Beloved, that's the same thing that God does with you when you are sanctified—Praise the Lord! He forgives your sins when you are saved, but you've still got the rottin' carcasses of the old nature deep in the well of your soul. That's why you don't have the victory and the power of the Holy Ghost in your life. You need to let God put down the bucket of sanctification and de-kittenize the well of your soul. Hallelujah! Oh, Hallelujah! You talk about a Second Blessing? When He makes you pure, you'll shout the victory all the way from this altar right through to the gates of Heaven-ah. Why not let God make you perfect in His sight tonight? If you are a Christian, there is no need for an invitation hymn. You should be so hungry for holiness that you would rush to this altar of prayer and never leave until you have the blessed assurance of a pure heart."

Pausing to let the truth sink in and sucking out of the guilt in every non-perfect heart, the preacher planted a conqueror's foot on the edge of the platform and eye-swept the territory of his conquest. Softly now, his voice dropped into a seductive invitation, "Won't y'all come?"

It was an offer that I could not refuse. With a lateral rush over the feet of my friends, I sped down the aisle and crumpled at a vacant kneeling spot four feet from the southern tip of the oaken arc. According to the script, this was to be the hallowed ground that my tears would stain, my fist would pound, and my eyes would check for that spot every time I testified. Here God was to bestow upon me the gift of His Spirit after dipping out the last bucket of my rotting nature. From here, I would arise as pure as God Himself.

On cue with my first step toward the altar, a supporting cast rushed to join me. Within seconds, I was surrounded by a cloud of praying witnesses, pleading counselors, and one-eye-through-the-fingers spectators. Like the accomplished conductor of a pick-up orchestra, I used a tearful prayer as a baton to start the music. "Oh, God, sanctify me . . . cleanse me . . . make me pure . . . I want to be holy."

In harmony, I heard, "Yes, Lord, answer Brother David's prayer." But, if you listened closely and sorted out the sounds, you could also detect the counterpoint,

"Tell Him what you need, Brother Dave."

"He knows what you need, Brother Dave."

"Once and for all, Lord,"

"Now or never, Lord."

"Oh, God, clean him out."

"Oh, God, fill him up."

"Let the purifying fire fall."

"Let the cleansing water flow."

"Praise God, I can feel Him coming."

"Praise God, He's already here."

The wave of prayer crested and fell into a trough of well-intended advice;

"Are you holding anything back?

"Are you hanging on?"

"Are you standing on the promises?

"Are you stepping out on the Word?'

"We'll stay all night if necessary."

"Why not right now?"

Momentum was building for another wave of prayer when the "de-kittenizing" evangelist crab-walked through the kneeling bodies and turned his attention to me. A massive hand encased my skull in a five-finger, fleshy cage. As he pressed down, the pain released a subconscious giggle, "Wow, when he lays on hands—HE LAYS ON HANDS!"

A sledgehammer blast pounded me back into submission, "WHATCHA AFTER, BOY?"

Thoroughly intimidated, I burst into tears again and blubbered, "I want to be sanctified." My aching head now became a crutch to lower the full weight of the 250-pound evangelist into a kneeling position. On the way down, he boomed again,

"OOOHHH, GAWD, You-all heard what this boy said . . . OOOHHHH, GAWD . . . You-all know what he needs . . . OOOHHHH, GAWD, OOOHHH, GAWD . . . Answer prayer, NOW! BURN OUT THE PRIDE IN HIS SOUL . . . now . . . now . . . NOW!"

As abruptly as he started, he stopped. Clamping his massive paw even tighter on my head, he pushed me down to lift himself up, "Ah know what's wrong." His confidence put a cork into every vial from which the sweet smell of prayer was wafting upward into the nostrils of God. Like seraphim with folded wings on Judgment Day, hushed saints awaited the verdict,

"Oh, oh," I thought, "What does he know? Did he see me shifting in my seat to get a better look at the hitched-up skirt of the girl across the aisle? Did he see me smirk at his bumpkin ways? Maybe he knows about the other sins in my life . . . "

None of these. Relief and surprise swept over me when the evangelist announced to the whole world, "It's pride . . . P-R-I-D-E . . . PRIDE in his curly hair." Ten large coarse fingers plowed, raked, and harrowed my hair, standing the curls on end and fuzzing up whatever was left of the part.

If there is virtue in a rumpled sacrifice, I qualified for instant sanctification. But how wrong he was. Just the week before, I had pled with my mother to get a brush-cut! Every jock in the school had straight hair standing on end with a help of a gummy gel and the status of an ever-present brush. So, to be one of the gang, I turned every trick to persuade my mother that I, too, needed a brush-cut. If there were any pride in my hair, it belonged without sin to my mother, who had encouraged every curl and pressed every wave when I was a baby.

Finally, Mother had relented. With an extra four-bits in hand, I made a macho march to the barber shop. "Let's have a brush-cut this time," I instructed the barber when my turn came.

"You can't get a brush-cut," he spoke with authority, "With your kinks and curls, it would never stand up."

"Not even if I train it with stick-um?"

"Not even if you train it with stick-um. I can cut it short, but you will never have a brush-cut."

His judgment rang with a finality that slumped me into the chair and prompted my resignation, "O.K. Cut it as short as you can."

Courage might have spurred me to stand up at the altar then and there to set facts straight. But courage comes hard when you are a 16-year-old bent over an altar, hemmed in by persevering saints, and shadowed by the evangelistic Hulk. Not only that, I was mad because he had messed up my hair and I was nursing some jealousy against this unsophisticated rube whose mousy mat was as straight as straw on a broomstick. More than that, I had been brainwashed by the bombardment of holiness preaching that pride was the root of sin. Preaching against pride had shaved my father's mustache, stripped off my mother's wedding band, and lengthened my sister's sleeves below the elbow. I too needed a symbolic lamb of pride to sacrifice on the altar. For all the wrong reasons, I conceded that he was right. Down went the head and up went the voice, "OH, LORD. TAKE AWAY MY PRIDE."

A dozen people collapsed on me in prayer and a hundred fingers reached for my head. From someplace above the crowd, an awful voice sounded the word of the rising tide to sing,

"The cleansing stream
I see, I see!
I plunge and O, it cleanseth me;
Oh, praise the Lord,
It cleanseth me,

Yes, cleanseth me."

An emotional surge gushed over my submissive soul and broke down every barrier of self-restraint. Light and free, I floated upward with hands, eyes and voice all saying at once, "Thank you, Lord." My audience spirited upward with me, transformed from groaning intercessors into jubilant shouters.

For the second time, I felt pure. But, in contrast with my conversion, I did not feel whole. I knew what I had to do. To prove my final victory over pride, I had to run around the Tabernacle. So, propelled by a shout, I broke out of the pack around the altar and took off up the aisle. At the back, a right-angle turn to the left took me into a crowd of non-praying malingerers who divided like the Red Sea at my shout, "Praise the Lord!" Another left-turn down the far aisle headed me back toward the altar and afforded me a peripheral glance at my entourage. "Aye-men Harry," the toothless, bald-headed, in-and-out convert who had taken Grandpa McKenna's place in the "Aye-men" corner, ran second and, far behind, came Sister Ida with a hanky-waving waddle. Everyone else stood cast in the concrete of disbelief.

One more left turn took me back to the spot at the altar where the run began. By now, only Brother Dan waved me home, and unless I was mistaken, Dad had a disappointed look on his face. Sanctification proved to be a hollow victory. After all the "feeshin'" we got the wrong kitten in the ole bucket.

13

Are You Washed in the Blood?

"Hey, did you hear that hot trombone? Let's go and listen." George, Terry and I were on our way to a Saturday night binge at the downtown Coke Bar when we heard the brilliant tone of a trombone leading the upbeat Salvation Army song,

> *"Are you washed in the blood?*
> *In the soul-cleansing blood of the Lamb?*
> *Are your garments spotless?*
> *Are they white as snow?*
> *Are you washed in the blood of the Lamb?"*

The sound of the music jellied my knees and clammied my hands. I had forgotten that this was street meeting night for The Evangelistic Mission Tabernacle. The band tooted, the make-shift choir squawked, Brother Dan bellowed and everyone else passed out tracts.

I had excused myself with a lie when Brother Dan asked me to play my trombone on the street corner. The truth was that I had no intention of compounding the stigma I felt among my high school buddies as a non-smoking, non-drinking, non-dancing, non-cardplaying, non-moviegoing guy who attended a strange church. So, I told Brother Dan that I had to work every Saturday night.

Now, the truth had caught up with me. Here I was on a collision course with the corner of my shame and in the tow of two high school seniors whose favor I desperately wanted. Even though they knew that my parents wouldn't let me play in the high school dance band or go to movies with them, they had no idea that I might be connected with the bunch of religious fanatics tooting, singing and passing out their propaganda on a street corner.

George, who played lead sax in the high school dance band, picked out the jazz-like qualities of Brother Dan's trombone long before we could see the semi-circle of the saints standing in the "No Parking" zone and facing toward the milling crowd around Ceccarelli's Café.

"Come on, let's go," George urged as he broke into a trot. Terry and I held back, he because of his strict Irish-Catholic upbringing and I because of my fear of exposure. Terry almost saved me when he looked ahead and spotted the fishers of men who formed a net on the corner through which no one could pass without receiving a Gospel tract or a martyr's tortured smile.

"Let's cross the street," he scoffed.

"Yeah, let's cross the street," I seconded the motion.

George, the undisputed leader in every teen-age dare, shot back. "No way. We can't hear the music over there." Compulsively drawn to the sound of the slide trombone, he stepped off the curb against the red light and plunged into the crowd on the other side of the street, sucking a scared Catholic and a self-incriminating Judas in his wake.

Bumping through the mass on the corner, I side-slipped up against the windows of the café with my face turned away from Brother Dan and his band. A tidal wave of nausea rolled through my stomach and crested in my throat as I imagined what Brother Dan would say if he saw me. "Bless God, it's Brother Dave. Come and tell us what God has done for you. Beloved, this young man is proof that you can live for Jesus even in high school."

My fears were groundless. Reveries of his own music swamped the consciousness of Brother Dan. Head up, eyes closed, through a full verse of song, he never noticed me. Relieved, but not yet free, I cast a furtive glance over Terry's shoulder to survey the free space through an opening in the crowd.

"Oh, no." Blocking the way at the other end of our obstacle course was "Aye-men Harry" offering a Gospel tract to George. Still mesmerized by the silken tones of Brother Dan's trombone, George unconsciously took the tract and stuffed it in his pocket without the slightest knowledge of his action. Terry, following closely behind George, brushed aside the outstretched hand offering him salvation and stepped around "Aye-men Harry" leaving me fully exposed and face-to-face with the same man who had once laid his hands on my head and prayed, "Save him, Lord."

Like a spiritual vending machine, "Aye-men Harry" ejected a tract at me, but then drew it back with a boisterous half-shout, "Well, Praise the Lord, Brother Dave. How ya' doin'?" Whatever "Open Sesame" I mumbled must have worked because "Aye-men Harry" ushered me past with a brotherly pat and aimed a tract at the more obvious sinner on my heels. Terry wasn't so easily fooled. Having picked up snatches of our exchange, he twisted his head around and struck out with the air of a Spanish Inquisitor, "What did he say to you? Do you know him?"

"Nah, just some old guy that Dad knows. Let's get going." Like Judas betraying his Lord, I found it easy to lie under pressure. At least Terry seemed satisfied, so we both pushed past the crowd to make our getaway.

George had other ideas. Turning left into the entrance of Flanagan's Drug Store, he halted us with a command couched in a compliment, "Man, is that a mellow trombone. Listen to that guy's glissando."

Once more, Terry pleaded, "Let's get out of here. I'm spooked."

Without missing a beat or taking his eyes off the trombone player, George grabbed Terry's arm and riveted him to the spot. I was free, but without a choice. Turning my back on my people, I turtled my head into the shell of my shoulders and professed genuine interest in the druggist's display of elastic stockings, sanitary napkins, and Carter's Little Liver Pills.

Brother Dan finally quit playing and started preaching. George lost interest immediately and so, with a wave of a point man directing a scouting party, he led our three-man safari on toward the Coke Bar. I found little consolation in the dimly-lit, high-backed booth just under the lazy, throbbing fan because George kept feeding nickel after nickel into the jukebox playing "I'm Getting Sentimental Over You" and trying to convince us that Brother Dan had a tone just as sweet as Tommy Dorsey.

****

Witnessing at a street meeting scored high on the scale of spirituality at The Evangelistic Mission Tabernacle. It stood just above telling someone face-to-face about your faith and just below a shouting spell in public. Try as I might, I flunked all three tests.

My face-to-face witness test came after I heard Brother Dan preach the text, "*Upon this rock, I will build My Church.*" In one fast, fell swoop, he obliterated the Roman Catholic argument that Christ established the papal lineage through Peter, whose name meant "a rock." Other strawmen fell. "The Rock" did not mean the established church or the resurrected Christ, but rather the personal experience of being saved and sanctified, or more precisely, The Gospel According to Brother Dan. Natural progression of Brother Dan's sermonic logic rolled the rock over one more time as he concluded that a Christian's testimony to a sinner was "The Rock" upon which the Kingdom of God would be built.

My own faulty logic then took over. "The Rock" meant two things to me. One was the fact of my experience in Christ that I had never shared with sinners. The other was Bob, the hero of our high school football team. Appropriately, or mis-appropriately, he was named "The Rock" because his last name was Marble.

"The Rock," captain of the State Champion football team, sat next to me in English class. Each Monday morning, he treated me to a cussingly-colorful, beer-by-beer, broad-by-broad, commentary on his week-end brawls. Already independent of his parents at the age of 17, he prided himself in the fact that he had never been inside a church, and to reinforce his distaste for religion, he laced his language with deliberate shots of profanity, vulgarity and blasphemy—all for my benefit.

One Sunday night at the Tabernacle, the wheel of conviction spun and stopped on my number. Guilty of sins done and good deeds undone, I followed the backslider's track to the mourner's bench and prayed clear through—again. Afterwards, one thought obsessed me. *I must witness to The Rock.* Before falling asleep that night, every gambit of my grand strategy was in place. Rising an hour early, I prayed for the opening to make my move. Then, arriving early for our first-period class, I would wait in ambush for "The Rock," and before he could cuss, my strategy was to open fire with the flurry of a Gatling gun, "Let me tell you what happened to me last night!"

Little prayers of thanks fell from my lips as the plan unfolded perfectly. "The Rock" made his grand entrance to the chatter of his football groupies, announced his presence by cracking his unmarked notepad on the desk, and weight-tested the scholar's chair with a "thud" of his case-hardened buttocks. Before he could breathe either "Whew!" or "Damn," my geyser burst. "Hi Rock, let me tell you what happened to me last night."

"Oh God, Man," he interrupted with the prerogative of the only man who could talk in the huddle other than the quarterback, "I was hammered all weekend. You should have been there. After the game Friday night, we all went to June's the Prune's house—you know her—and emptied every six-pack her old man had. What a blast!"

Good Grief! Charlie Brown was still 10 or 15 years from creation, but I knew then how he felt when Lucy, Linus and he were lying on their backs one summer day tracing images in the clouds above their heads,

"Over there, I see the profile of the poet Keats," Lucy began.

" . . . and to the north, I see a map of the Caribbean," Linus chips in.

"Yes" Lucy continues, "If you look closely you can see the image of St. Paul as he attends the martyrdom of St. Stephen."

"What about you, Charlie Brown, what do you see?" Lucy asks.

Snapping up to a sitting position, Charlie's big circle eyes grow large and sad, "Well, I was going to say that I saw a ducky and a horsey, but I've changed my mind."

Similarly, "The Rock's" snapshot of his lost weekend erased my well-rehearsed theological soliloquy that I had memorized to sound like this: "Jesus saved me from my sins last night. I was lost and going to hell. But I bowed at an altar of prayer and now I am a new creature in Christ Jesus. Rock, wouldn't you like to be saved too?"

The testimony stuck in my throat. I was overpowered. So, when my turn came, I settled for a religious joke. "Last night I heard a good one about a preacher and a bear . . . Have you heard it?"

"The Rock" grunted, so I went on. "Well, this old preacher went bear hunting. He saw a bear and raised his gun to shoot. But then, he got bear fever and froze on the trigger. The bear turned and treed the preacher. Higher and higher he climbed with the bear close behind. When he reached the top limb with no place to go, he began to pray, 'Lord, Lord, if you cain't he'p me, for heben's sake, don't he'p that bear.'"

My Gospel blimp sputtered on takeoff, but I didn't expect it to be shot down. "That's not for me, man," Rock's verbal buckshot punctured my air balloon. Thud! As far as I was concerned, if Christ wanted to build His Church, He'd have to find another "Rock."

Stand-up testimonies in church came easier for me, that is, until the pressure built for a public demonstration. Perhaps in betrayal of my future interest in research, I devised a 10-point scale for public demonstration:

Spiritual Rating	Type of Demonstration
1	Hand in air while seated
2	Standing alone with hand in air
3	Walking aisle, waving hand

4	Marching in aisle behind band
5	Running around the church
6	Marching outside behind the band
7	Prancing on the altar
8	Running over pews
9	Turning cartwheels before the altar
10	Shouting down the center line on Michigan Avenue

Except for one regrettable trip around the church, I never let myself go past "1." Even when the Tabernacle band marched around the aisles or out-of-doors around the church, I sat huddled in the orchestra loft with "Buddha Rollie," our red-faced clarinetist, with my eyes glued on the 2/4 music,

> *"Onward, Christian soldiers, Marching as to war,*
> *With the cross of Jesus, Going on before!*
> *Christ, the Royal Master, Leads against the foe;*
> *Forward into battle, See His banners go."*

If I am to play my trombone when the saints go marching in, I'll have to have an angel alongside holding my music and turning the pages.

For others, high marks on the scale of public demonstrations became a competitive challenge. Many scored "6" by marching behind the band when it circled the church, but "7s," "8s" and "9s" were reserved for the evangelistic acrobats who danced on the altar, raced over the pews, and turned cartwheels across the front of the church. Some of the evangelistic circuit-riders brought eye-popping stories of shouting spells on Main Street (equivalent of our Michigan Avenue), but no one had ever scored a "10" in the Tabernacle.

One night it happened. "Aye-men Harry" and "Shouting Shirley" were vying for the honors of letting the world know that if sinners can yell at ballgames, Christians can cheer for Jesus. Sadly, an overweight outcast in the local high school, "Shouting Shirley" got her kicks and attention by yelling, "I don't need no ballgames. I say, 'HOORAY FOR JESUS.'"

"Aye-men Harry" caught the cue, jumped to his feet, and yelled back across the Tabernacle, "HOORARY FOR JESUS."

Back and forth the sound and the pitch rose until "Shouting Shirley" surprised everyone by breaking into a run down the aisle. Picking up speed as she waddled, she shot out through the double doors in the back, gyrating to her shout, "HOORAY FOR JESUS."

Brother Dan signaled for a song as if nothing had happened, but even he must have wondered what happened to "Shouting Shirley" for the next ten eternal minutes. Suspense gave way to worry and I heard my mother whisper to my father, "Don't you think that someone should find out if Shirley's all right?"

No sooner said than done. The same door that had disgorged Shirley burst open again to the hoarse yell, "HOORAY FOR JESUS." As if needing to unwind, "Shouting Shirley" circled the church once again, stopped to get her breath, and then told how she had become a "fool for Jesus" by running down the center line of Michigan Avenue, commandeering every car with her Jesus yell.

For a while, street-shouting proved to be a new spiritual high. "Aye-men Harry" also gave it a whirl. On the third try, a neighbor called the police to press the charge that we were disturbing the peace. Two blue-coats stepped through the double doors and beckoned Brother Dan to the back. When he returned to the pulpit, he treated the encounter like a morality play between Good and Evil by declaring, "Bless God, we may be arrested, but when the Spirit takes control, we must obey God rather than man."

Nonetheless, shouting spells on Michigan Avenue became extinct and I suspect that everyone was relieved, including Jesus. After all, He keeps no scoreboard on spiritual shenanigans and certainly He suffers more fools than He can ever use.

14

Blessed Assurance

"THUS SAITH THE LORD" exploded in the chamber of Brother Dan's pursed mouth, smoked along the barrel of his target-picking finger, and scored hit after hit among his awestruck victims. "A cigarette is a devil stick with a fire on one end and a fool on the other-ah. Hungry kids are crying themselves to sleep tonight-ah, while their fathers booze it up in some bar. Young-ah men are going straight to hell in the arms of floozies from the dance floors of our high schools-ah."

One by one, the Five Fundy Sins—smoking, drinking, dancing, card-playing and theater-going—were set as stationary targets and shot down in a rapid-fire, verbal volley. Spinning the cylinder with the dare of a Russian at roulette, the Gospel Gunslinger fired again and again.

"CRACK—painted nails poking out of toeless shoes do not show your pretty skin . . . they show your ugly soul!"

"CRACK—Some of you mothers should be ashamed of putting dresses on your daughters that are so short . . . that they show their little. . .(Brother Dan caught himself on the borderline of a barnyard word. . .but the people urged him on by pressing forward in their seats like an audience at a Johnny Carson show. Their body language seemed to tease out the question, "How short are they?")" . . . so short that you can see their little . . . little . . . crotch!"

Brother Dan crossed the line of common sense in public utterance. Heads dropped and throats gulped, but not with effect on the ranting preacher. He savored his ability to shock and fired again:

"CRACK! The Lord is looking down on some of the low-cut dresses that you women are wearing . . . and He doesn't like what He sees . . . (only born comics and dirty old men chuckled at the misfire. Unintentionally, Brother Dan had contributed one of the world's funniest one-liners to the repertoire of stand-up comedians.)

"ZAP!, ZAP!, ZAP! Successive slugs struck closer home—sleeveless dresses, plucked eyebrows, wedding rings, Sunday newspapers—nothing was said about turning over new Buicks every year, which was Brother Dan's most visible vice, or about high-fashion hats, which may been Sister Helen's only edge over Sister Bonney in competition for his favors.

Sooner or later, Brother Dan's bullets took on names. Just as he had singled out Cousin Dolly for her earrings, he had the audacity to aim his hollow-point slugs so precisely that when they hit, everyone knew the target and saw the messy wound. Fear kept the souls of The Evangelistic Mission Tabernacle from open rebellion. Underneath their cowardice, however, the assaults accumulated until they were forced into choices. They could backslide; they could change churches; or they could continue to suffer in silence. No one had confronted Brother Dan except Sister Lola. . .until one day!

Brother Paul, a hard-working and creative transplant from another revivalist sect, volunteered to be the Superintendent for the Young People's Society. Immediately, he and his wife began to invent activities for the dance-less, movie-less, and card-less teens in the Tabernacle. Brother Dan glowed and cooed over their spiritual leadership for the young people when Brother Paul and his wife marched down the aisle one Sunday evening with twenty teenagers in tow. The small army created its own "Aye-men" corner in a section of seats that were right up front.

Trouble began to brew when Brother Paul and his wife extended their influence with the young people into ball games, ice-cream socials, and a Saturday night party that violated the Sabbath by twelve minutes. Empty seats and sleepy heads told the story. Brother Dan could not stand the competition. So, in the evening service of the same Sunday, behind the formidable fortress of the huge oak pulpit, he invoked his condemnation:

". . . and while I am on the subject, we must be aware of false prophets who will try to woo the tender souls of our children into the Kingdom of God for fun and games . . . but-ah, by the authority of the Word of God, let me warn you that there are no substitutes for the old-fashioned, sin-forsaking, Spirit-filled, straight and narrow way-ah. Our young people need God, not games . . . and the false prophets who lead them astray must face the uncompromising truth of God's Holy Word."

An unseen finger pushed the ejector button under Brother Paul's seat. Simultaneous with his physical rising, he threw out the challenge, "Brother Dan, if you mean me, say so . . ."

Shock waves paralyzed the congregation. The preacher turned into a blue-serge pillar with a blood-drained alabaster face. Eyeballs locked in an impasse between an immovable object and an irresistible force.

Then, into the dead space came a squeaky voice pinched by rage: "I feel the same way. Last week you preached against my wife and I'm not going to take it anymore. We don't need a dictator."

Enemy to the right of him, enemy to the left of him, Brother Dan's eyes betrayed a rare show of fear. Momentarily, he slid his gaze from a fix on Brother Paul to identify the other Judas. It was Brother Milan, the only man of modest wealth in the whole congregation. Brother Dan stood squared up with the pulpit, his defiant jaw jutting out to accent the black beads of eyes now sunk in cynical slits:

"Right," Brother Paul broke in again, "We need a meeting of all the members of the church to make some decisions . . ."

"Yes," Brother Milan picked up the verbal baton that his cohort had handed him, "We've got to make decisions . . . including who will be our pastor!"

The Rubicon passed under these words. Knowing that he could not turn back, Brother Milan strode toward the altar, not be repent, but to plead with the congregation like a cheerleader in the Roman colosseum. Some thumbs went up; most thumbs went down. Brother Milan, catching the sense of the meeting, finished with an ultimatum directed at my father, the Chairman of the Board: "The next time I appear in this church, it will be to decide whether we want a dictator or a pastor."

Up the aisle he went, followed by his wife and family. Up the other side, Brother Paul led a procession of his family, picking up a few scattered loyalists on the way out. No one else dared to move. Brother Dan could only stutter, "I . . . I . . . I preach against sin, not people. God has said that His Word is a two-edged sword. It cuts both ways. I must preach the Word, no matter who it hurts."

On that defiant note, Brother Dan resorted to a benediction from rote memory: *"May the love of God, the grace of our Lord Jesus Christ, and the Communion of the Holy Spirit be with you now and forever more. Aye-men."*

Piece by piece, the Body of Christ left the Tabernacle. Sanctimonious "God bless ya's" and irrelevant "How yah doin's" were forgotten as the saints scattered. Everyone wanted to put as much distance as possible between themselves and the reality of a confrontation in which someone had to lose. A fast exit seemed to be the best escape.

No hint of the conflict marred our Sunday afternoon dinner. Yet, just beneath the surface, tension mounted in our minds as time closed in on the evening service. We, the young, were ready to welcome a donnybrook to replace "The Inner Sanctum" radio mystery that we had to sacrifice at the seven o'clock hour. Our hopes fluttered and fell when neither Brother Milan nor Brother Paul showed up for the service. A visitor would never have guessed that turmoil had torn apart the morning worship. Hands were clapped and waved during repeated refrains of "Jesus Saves," testimonies glowed in the warmth of the Spirit's visitation, feverish prayers carried unnamed sinners into the mercy of God, and Brother Dan attacked only the devil by sticking to his text, "Get thee behind me, Satan."

Judgment fell the next morning. Before 7:00 a.m. our telephone rang. A tear-choked voice blurted out, "Is your radio on? Have you heard the news? BROTHER MILAN IS DEAD. He was killed in a truck accident at four o'clock this morning."

A grisly story followed. To get a jump on his competition in the fruit and vegetable business, Brother Milan had left home in the dark of Monday morning to head for the Farmer's Market in Detroit. His genius for turning a profit on a shoestring operation thus contributed to his death. Driving a cast-off milk truck complete with a stand-up steering wheel and sliding doors that would not close, he challenged the zero visibility of the pre-dawn darkness and an early morning fog. Brother Milan's fatal error was to assume that he drove alone through the familiar crossroads between his home and the highway. Intersections one, two, and three passed under the wheels of his truck as he picked up speed and confidence. The fourth intersection became his final cross. Another driver, operating under the same assumption, broadsided his milk truck through the driver's open door, propelling Brother Milan through the opposite side to a skull-shattering smash on the roadway. An instant later, his milk truck administered the *coup-de-grace* by rolling on top of him.

Violent death telegraphed a message of judgment to every member of The Evangelistic Mission Tabernacle. "BROTHER MILAN DEFIED GOD'S MAN. STOP. GOD BROUGHT JUSTICE. END."

Yet, at the funeral three days later, Brother Dan ushered Brother Milan through the gates of heaven without the slightest show of hostility or hypocrisy. No one who shuddered at the sound of the widow's hysterical weeping will ever forget the eerie calm that settled over her during Brother Dan's graveside solace,

> *"Well done, good and faithful servant. Enter into the joys of the Lord. Aye-men and Aye-men."*

God's grace and Brother Dan's generosity appeared to be inseparable. After all, even Caesar turned a thumb up once in a while.

15

Yield Not to Temptation

"AFTER THE SERVICE, AH want all you boys who are here-ah in the House of the Lord to pick up one of the Gospel tracts that ah left on the rack at the back of the sanctuary."

My sex education at The Evangelistic Mission Tabernacle had begun. Earlier, I had heard about Hollywood harlots, dance-floor doxies, and passionate priests. Later, I would learn about homosexual evangelists and adulterous preachers. In between these revelations, the evils of sex had been equated with women who sported short skirts, low necklines, bobbed hair, toeless shoes and painted lips. Men were gloriously exempt. Still, it didn't relieve the guilt that I felt over a growing urge that wouldn't go away.

The invitation of the itinerant evangelist to pick up one of his Gospel "tracks" brought the problem into focus. Although he had sermonized on sex, not once did he deal with the infectious disease that was festering at the heart of the Tabernacle. Instead, he chose to dangle over Hell the young boys in his congregation who were teetering on both sides of puberty. His sermon set the stage. Using the outline, "The Lust of the Eyes, The Lust of the Flesh, and The Pride of Life," the drawling Southern Discomforter walked his fingers through the yellowed pages of sexual sins. His homiletical triad lacked only the visual aid of three monkeys posing to illustrate, "See no sex, Feel no sex, Think no sex." Negative followed negative until the evangelist concluded with the invitation for every young man to stop at the back for some free, follow-up literature.

Curiosity caused a line-up at the bookshelf just inside the double doors. One glance at the smudgy, black headlines, "The Sin of Onan" (Genesis 38:9–10) led me to stuff it in my pocket like a shoplifter in a department store. Bedtime reading seemed more appropriate. So, an hour later, I was deep down in my covers with a bed lamp shining into the cavern I had often created for reading comic books after the time for lights out. In that setting of subterfuge, I met Onan, the tragic Old Testament character whom God struck dead for the sin of spilling his seed on the ground. Without so much as a nod toward the historical context of the Scripture, the author of the tract matched Onanism with masturbation and proceeded to describe the act in a step-by-step, do-it-yourself manual.

For a boy coming into puberty without the benefit of the birds and the bees, the tract painted some full-color fantasies of things to come. I read on. Splat! My fantasies fell before the judgment of God. Onan was slain in one slashing stroke because spilling his seed was an unpardonable sin against nature, marriage and God. "Why then," I asked, "Doesn't God strike dead the heirs of Onan today?" The author anticipated my question. God still slays the sons of Onan, he wrote, but the death is slower. Young men today are struck blind, dumb, insane and impotent. To support his argument, medical statistics and doctors' quotations were lined up like sentinels ready to catch the wayward boy in a crossfire of deadly condemnation. When I turned out the light that night, collapsed the cavern of my blankets, and rolled over to sleep, I took into my nightmare the fear of death for the thought of sex. Nimbus clouds of black and foreboding guilt would hang over my soul for years to come.

Later, I learned why preaching at The Evangelistic Mission Tabernacle never dealt with the Biblical view of the beauty and sanctity of sex. The subject was too threatening. Peripheral skirmishes into women's styles, Hollywood movies, and social dancing served as decoys for sin at the rotting core.

Sooner or later, it had to happen. One Sunday morning during testimony time, Sister Lola, a new and comely convert, stood up and screamed across the Tabernacle, "IF I CAN'T HAVE HIM, SHE CAN'T EITHER!"

A three-sided sex scandal blew into the open. Sister Lola, jealous, jilted and uninhibited, stabbed her accusation to the opposite corner of the church where Sister Helen demurely sat with her sleepy-eyed husband. At the sound of the words, however, she looked up to see the finger pointing directly at her. Their eyes met and flashed the hate that is reserved for jilted lovers and sexual competitors. In between, but just out of the line of fire, Brother Dan's face flushed with the dilemma of being the private lover and public referee at the same time. If there was a fourth party, it was Brother Dan's wife, seated at the piano with a look of disbelief, but not with the shock that one expects for a wife betrayed.

To understand the volcanic rage seething to the surface in the public confrontation between Sister Lola and Sister Helen, the thread of history must be pulled through from the time of Brother Dan's arrival at the Tabernacle as a white-hot Lancelot to the moment of his exposure as a red-hot Lothario. No one questioned the interconnected couples characterized by sheepish men and lionish women from Indiana who migrated lock, stock and barrel behind Brother Dan. To the contrary, their decision was extolled as a modern example of Abraham who " . . . *went out, not knowing where he went.*" Tabernacle-ites welcomed them with open arms because their sturdy Indiana stock meant conservative convictions, faithful church attendance, and generous giving. The bonus was their musical flair—every one of them sang or played an instrument so that the musical ministry of the Tabernacle was multiplied and upgraded by the Holstein Family Singers and their variety of solos, duets, trios and a mixed quartet.

Most of the Holstein women were built like their name, strong and bulky. Sister Helen was the exception. Although expensive two-piece suits kept her shape a mystery, her face spoke for total beauty. A blush of red on China cheeks accented Madonna-like features. Either lipstick or mascara would have violated the natural beauty of her lips and eyes. Soft, brown hair framed her face with gentle waves that could not be tamed, even with a pull-back bun that she wore to meet Tabernacle standards.

Despite her natural beauty, Sister Helen betrayed one trace of vanity. She loved the highest fashion in flowered hats. For her, every Sunday was an Easter parade. For us, the lusty gang of adolescent upstarts who slouched in the back row, the only salvation in being forced to attend church was to place bets on the size, shape and style of Sister Helen's latest creation. We christened each hat with a name. A somber, blue pillbox got dubbed "Joan of Arc" because it seemed to prepare Sister Helen for either war or martyrdom. "Hedda Hopper" grew out of a basket of assorted flowers that turned the wearer into a walking bouquet. "Mona Lisa" became our choice for a wide-brimmed, white-encircling straw that spun a halo around her angelic face. A drooping, mannish "Greta Garbo" spoke for itself. But all of us waited for the rare moment when Sister Helen sported her black caballero model with its flat, horizontal brim that shadowed her eyes with intrigue. At any moment, we expected "Ava Gardner" to crack a bull whip and stomp a bolero once again.

Not only did Sister Helen's hats become a game with us, but her personality did as well. One time we tried to imagine her holding narcissistic devotions before her dressing mirror on Sunday morning while waiting for the revelation that would determine her hat for the day. "Do I want to appear as a saint or a sinner? An innocent beauty or a mystery woman?" Whatever answer she got, a special flower always graced each creation. Even her Spanish model sported a black rose.

Brother Roland, her husband, served as a foil for the ludicrous. Imagine a red-faced Buddha looking out of blinking-toad eyes with a round head topped by spit-slicked hair parted front and center along what looked like an old war wound. In humorous contrast to his stylish wife, Brother Roland always appeared in church in an ill-fitting shirt and flowered tie that pointed downward to an overlapping belly and an invisible belt. At one time, his two suits—one blue and one brown—had been good merchandise, probably chosen according to his wife's taste with the hope that clothes would make the man. She lost. Brother Roland was a man who unmade his clothes. Perpetually unpressed, the suit bulged beyond buttons at the belly-level and sagged in surrender over ostrich legs that were pegged into hook-and-eye work shoes. Perhaps the battered work shoes also symbolized his one allowable point of rebellion against his dominant, fashion-conscious wife.

Seen together, they were the original odd couple. When the Holstein family migrated north along the trail blazed by Brother Dan, they left behind homes, farms, and land. Brother Roland had the most to lose. He had to forfeit a bundle of sweet equity in a farm that needed just a year or two of tender loving care to break even. The move caused a double loss. Not only did Brother Roland's dream evaporate when he couldn't sell his Indiana farm for its potential value, but he had to become low man on an automobile assembly line in order to survive in the new setting. Sister Helen's vanity must have dipped low when they had to settle for a farm cottage with a few acres for her husband's garden, a pen for his pigs, and a barn big enough for a cow or two. As luck would have it, Brother Roland's lot at the factory fell on the swing shift from 3:00 to 11:00 p.m. Later on, when he gained the seniority to claim a day job, he refused. The swing-shift was perfect for the cycle of evening work, late night sleep, and daytime farming.

Evidently another swinger took advantage of the afternoon shift. Although the details disappeared in the secret strategy that brings lovers together, hearsay with a bit of imagination fills out the story. Brother Dan made frequent pastoral calls on the lonely Sister Helen. Rumor had it that folks in the neighboring farm could set their watches by Brother Roland's functional Ford coasting past on the way to work with plenty of time to spare and Brother Dan's finned and chromed Buick speeding ahead of a cloud of dust as if on the way to an urgent pastoral call.

No one would have known what happened during the years of those clandestine trysts if Brother Dan's sexual appetite had not been whetted again by the sight of the voluptuous young convert, Sister Lola. She too, suffered from the handicap of a husband whose level of aspiration remained in a small Appalachian mining town even after they had discovered the higher wages and greater opportunities of the urban North. One child sealed their shaky teenage marriage, a girl who seemed to symbolize the moment when Sister Lola screamed at her boorish husband, "Don't you ever touch me again!"

Through her daughter, Sister Lola lived out her frustrated desire to be a beauty queen. The child jumped into puberty before her mother was thirty, so together, they shared the frills and fads of bargain-counter fashions. On the daughter, the styles and colors were forgivable, but on the mother, they were cardinal sins. In stark contrast to the stylish Sister Helen, Sister Lola modeled lacy purple crepes with scooping necklines, even for funerals. But, as a new convert in the Tabernacle, she was permitted a "grace period" until she got the light through Brother Dan's scalding sermons on women's dress.

Strange, but Brother Dan quit preaching on dress when Sister Lola got saved. Other women of the Tabernacle remained in uniform, but Sister Lola went scot-free. For the boys in the back row, she was renamed "Daisy Mae." Just a little imagination dropped her frilly, scooped neckline off the shoulder, shredded her dress up to the thigh, bared her feet, unpinned her hair, and set her running with a seductive giggle through a hillside hollow with Mountain Magoo in hot pursuit.

Even when she testified, she wriggled. To be candid, she oozed sex and her new-found spirituality only added to the ooze. When other women in the Tabernacle testified, their lumpy bodies proved that they had given up the flesh in favor of the spirit. Not so with Sister Lola. With a soft, affected drawl, she breathed life into lust once again.

Only Brother Dan possessed the power to act out the thoughts that Sister Lola provoked in men. Slowly, but deliberately, his pastoral calls shifted sisters. Sister Lola, a gullible soul for whom sexuality was the only leverage she had ever known, slid willingly into his clutches, at first under the ruse of pastoral attention, but later under the charm of a smooth and accomplished lover. Alas, that was Brother Dan's error. Sister Helen's intelligence told her that she had had the best of two worlds—the security of a faithful husband and the excitement of a clandestine lover. Quite the opposite, Sister Lola had nothing to lose. Her husband offered neither stability nor status. Her daughter was a competitor in a beauty contest that youth was destined to win. Lack of subtlety was Sister Lola's other handicap. Either limited intellect or minimal wisdom kept her from seeing the waves of repercussion from a public confession of her role as Brother Dan's "other mistress." Only one thought obsessed her. She must have her man at all costs!

Whether by chance or choice, Sister Lola discovered Brother Dan's long-term, late afternoon love affair with Sister Helen. So, the next time he came for her favors, she acted out her jealous impulses in a demand that he make a choice between mistresses. Ultimatums were alien to Brother Dan. How would he handle this woman? His cause was far short of righteous and his case would never stand up in the court of public opinion. Only his iron-clad ministerial authority remained. True to form, the look on his face passed from lover's charm to prophet's steel. Without naming his prey, Sister Lola was denounced as a scarlet woman who had used the guile of Satan to seduce an innocent man of God. Then, with unmatched gall, he prayed for her deliverance from the sin of sex.

Sister Lola swallowed the spiritual hemlock. She confessed sex as her "thorn in the flesh" at the altar the next Sunday night. Brother Dan himself prayed her "clear through".

Like Constantine's army who held the tip of their swords out of the water when they were baptized as Christians, Sister Lola kept the point of her jealousy out of the cleansing in her spiritual washing. Three days later, Brother Dan felt the sharpened edge at his throat. As the fleeting word would have it, Sister Lola drove to the countryside and stationed herself at a strategic spot on a side-road leading to Sister Helen's home. Sure enough, her suspicion was justified when she spotted a racy Buick emerging from a cloud of dust, obviously on time for a synchronized rendezvous.

No more private prayers or humiliating altar calls for Sister Lola. With nothing to lose, she decided on a public exposé during testimony the next Sunday night. How many times she rehearsed her accusatory speech before the mirror at home during the next four days, no one knows. Her hearers knew, however, that it was a beauty. Intensity even tightened her natural wriggle that rippled from a toss of her head to the hitch of her hips. Without a word, she eyeballed Brother Dan and then swept left and right, pausing only to anchor the corners of her waiting audience. Assured of undivided attention, she retraced her line of sight back to the preacher as if seeking permission to begin. When none came, she tossed her head once more in defiance and turned her appeal to the people.

"You-all remember last Sunday night. Ah went to the altar and asked God to forgive me for being in love with another man . . . (Timely tears glistened in her eyes) . . . God did forgive me . . ." (like the woman caught in the act of adultery, her head fell as if to await the stones).

"AYE-MEN, Sister Lola, yes, He did." Easy atonement had slipped from Brother Dan's facile tongue. His error was fatal. Instead of soothing a sinful soul, his impulses poured flammable fluid on an open flame. Sister Lola's repentant head snapped up, her black eyes flashed hate, and her lips curled back as if to bare fangs.

"Yes, He did," she snarled, "But He did not forgive THE MAN!" By her direction and inflection of voice, only a simpleton would not have known that Brother Dan himself was "THE MAN." "And," Lola sped on, "He didn't forgive THAT WOMAN!"

A finger now led all eyes across two aisles and into the section of seats where Sister Helen sat with her husband and among her family. No one would have guessed that she was the other adulterer. Everything about her exuded innocence—a simple, blue-veiled tiara head piece, a swept back hairdo that ended in a prayerful bun, and of course, the big doe eyes of a modern Madonna. If she had not dropped her head in shame, Sister Lola might have been indicted for perjury. Too late. A saint had fallen, condemned by a drop of the head and a flutter of the eyes. A scarlet "A" had been dropped around the neck of Sister Helen.

Out of the well of hate, then, came the explosive charge, "IF I CAN'T HAVE HIM, SHE CAN'T EITHER!" Once again, the ancient insight proved true. "*Heaven has no rage like love to hate turned; nor hell no fury like a woman scorned.*" (Proverb by William Congreve. Neither biblical nor Shakespearean.)

Whatever happened next is lost in the fog of faulty memory and uncontrolled gossip. Common to hearsay is the report that Brother Dan gathered his wits, invoked his pastoral authority, and preached a sermon on forgiveness that exonerated both women.

I lost my hero. No longer did I see Billy Sunday and Tommy Dorsey reflected in the image of Brother Dan. Instead, I saw Elmer Gantry, the evangelist in Sinclair Lewis's novel who preached old-time religion and seduced women with his charms. He too played the trombone.

I also lost my church. When Sister Lola vented her jealous rage with the scream, "IF I CAN'T HAVE HIM, SHE CAN'T EITHER!" it was the beginning of the end for The Evangelistic Mission Tabernacle.

16

When the Roll Is Called Up Yonder

AFTER BROTHER MILAN'S TRAGIC death, mutiny in the Tabernacle became a lost cause. Brother Paul disappeared from the ranks and surfaced again as the Sunday School Superintendent of another independent church where women bobbed their hair and men muffled their shouts. Like the two-edged sword that Brother Dan yielded, judgment slashed two ways. For many months, his sermons were tenderized, cooled and watered down. Whether security or fear moderated his attack, no one could tell. One thing was sure. No one questioned his authority again without considering the consequences. No one, that is, but me.

A spoonful of innocence mixed with scoops of deceit cooked up my one-man revolt the following New Year's Eve. Initially, I didn't intend to flaunt Brother Dan's authority or run the risk of being crushed by God's mailed fist. Yet, in all candor, I was ready to try any ruse that might reduce my five-hour sentence to the confines of the annual New Year's Watch Night marathon that began at 7:30 p.m. and never finished before 12:30 the next morning. Agony accompanied the pain because I secretly yearned to be dancing on my feet rather than praying on my knees at the stroke of midnight. Watch Night service meant that I had to sacrifice the Homecoming Queen, a pagan by Tabernacle definition, into the arms of my arch-rival, who shared the reputation with my girlfriend as the school's best dancers.

Yes, I was a Christian leading two lives. On Sunday I lived as a straightlaced Tabernacle-ite with a lockstep schedule of worship services and its attendant role of testimony, singing, and prayer. Throughout the week, however, I lived as a high school senior and a leader in band, debate, student government, and tennis. And my heart belonged to a black-haired beauty who would be condemned because of red lips and a reputation for jitterbugging. My non-dancing and non-movie-going stance limited our affection to holding hands while walking home from school and saying "Good-bye" with a discrete kiss. Still, the Senior Yearbook gave special attention to our relationship as a well-known "item" among our high school peers.

Perhaps you can see why of all the religious wrappings that bound me, the Watch Night service turned out to be the final twist and tug that mummified my soul. Too scared to skip the service and too smart to feign sickness, I resorted to a self-justifying, spiritual reason for my absence. As the President of the Young People's Society, I had the responsibility to plan the program for the New Year's Day Rally. Young people from all of the offshoots of The Evangelistic Mission Tabernacle, coincidentally pastored by brothers, sisters or brothers-in-law of Brother Dan, gathered together in competition with the Rose Bowl.

After writing the script for the program, I decided to add some visual flair to the narrative by building a silver-foil cross emblazoned by the red letters spelling out the theme:

J E **S** U S
A
V
E
S

Skillful procrastination brought me to the time for the Watch Night service with a half-finished cross. "Oh," I responded sanctimoniously to the church-time call from my father, "I've got to finish my cross."

Who could deny such an unselfish sacrifice? One look at the spiritual promise of my work and Dad agreed; "Okay. Come as soon as you can."

Three dawdling hours later, I took up my cross and followed my father. After planting it in the center of the basement platform for the edification of the youthful pretenders to sainthood who would gather there the next day, I climbed the stairs to the upper room. Smugly, I slipped through the swinging doors of the sanctuary by timing my entrance with the third season of prayer. One could always count upon anonymity when "Every knee is bowed, every head is down, and every eye is closed" . . . or so I thought.

Brother Dan must have had a radar scan on his worshippers so that I appeared as a late-coming blip on his screen. At twenty minutes to midnight, he took the text for his second sermon of the evening. My best-laid plans went the way of all the efforts of mice and men when Brother Dan rolled the sweet morsel of his revised text over his tongue, "Forsake not the assembling of yourselves together, for such is the WILL OF THE LORD." The will of Whom? I soon found out.

After a disarming warmup, Brother Dan's face began to puff red, his eyes ignited with holy hate, his steps became angry stomps, and his trigger finger quivered in the air just before it snapped into place—pointing directly at me! "You think that you are called to preach, do you? God cannot use a lily-livered pantywaist who has never done a speck of work in his life."

I was the only one I knew who professed the call to preach, but what's this business about a lily-livered pantywaist?

"You talk about going away to Bible college to learn the Word of God? That isn't what you need. You need-ah to get your pretty patties into some honest grease. . .You need to bump your head against this old-fashioned mourner's bench and pray through. That's what you need."

I alone had filed an application for Bible college, but pretty patties?

"You pretend to be a leader, do you? What kind of example are you? Playing around when you should be in the House of God?

Let me tell you, God has no room for kiddies who play at religion . . . He needs MEN . . . He needs LEADERS who follow His will . . . Forsake not the assembling . . . "

BONG. . .!

Saved by the bell. At the stroke of midnight and in the middle of Brother Dan's tirade, the bells in the belfry began to ring and a voice broke out with the New Year's tradition, "All Hail the Power of Jesus' Name." Brother Dan had no choice but to end his preaching and join the chorus. With whistles and firecrackers as the background he then ordered his shouting saints to be on their knees at the long, long altar. A fourth season of prayer and five verses of "Blest Be the Tie that Binds" (the counter-hymn to "Auld Lang Syne") led to an elongated benediction that spanned the year gone by and covered every contingency for the year ahead. Neither bells nor whistles, neither prayer nor hymn, neither tear nor handshake soothed my troubled soul. Guilt was now gone. In its place boiled a fighting rage, provoked by the perspective that Brother Dan had taken a "cheap shot."

How did he know that I dallied with my cross to avoid the long Watch Night Service? Except for the underlying guilt and the shock of his uncanny knowledge, I would have walked out of the service, even at the risk of being struck dead. Such a thought passed quickly as I imagined myself being added to the repertoire of death-bed stories for traveling evangelists. True to form, Brother Dan or one of his buddies would swoon, "Dave was a brilliant young man, one of the most popular in his high school. God called him to preach the Gospel, and like David of old, anointed him with His Spirit. He became President of the Young People's Society . . . He planned to attend Bible college-ah . . . but . . . but . . . but dearly beloved . . . he began to toy with the Holy Spirit. Oh, at first, it was just a small thing . . . like coming late to church-ah . . . but from then on, Satan nipped at his soul until his ear became heavy when The Spirit spoke and his heart-ah became hard when The Spirit led. Who knows when he passed the deadline? Who knows when the Holy Spirit became so grieved that He never spoke to him again? It happened at a Watch Night Service. A Man of God preached the whole Truth under the inspiration of the Spirit-ah. Like the prophet Nathan, he pointed his finger at Dave and declared, 'THOU ART THE MAN!'"

Stoking the heat under my collar were thoughts about the cowardice I had shown under fear of Brother Dan. How ridiculous I must have appeared, even to the Tabernacle-ites, when I arrived for the Friday night evangelistic service in full-dress uniform as first chair trombonist for the high school marching band. Timing my exit from the service to coincide with the end of the first half of the football game, I ran several blocks to the field just in time to take my place on the "Eyes Right" corner of the marching band for its half-time performance. My privilege then permitted me to remain for the rest of the football game before walking home alone while my friends headed for damnation at the Dime Dance that always followed.

Equally ridiculous, I remembered the picture that had been taken of the high school tennis team for the yearbook. Tennis qualified as a sport in which I could participate because the matches were all played in the afternoon. Energetic, but mediocre, I stuck it out on the #2 doubles team until the honor of co-captain fell my way by attrition. But, as luck would have it, a tight-bunned, long-skirted, and full-hosed high school sister from the Tabernacle saw me practicing in tennis shorts. Somehow, she spread the word of my immodesty until it reached Brother Dan. Sure enough, tennis shorts became the "appearance of evil" in next Sunday's sermon so that my mother took me shopping for long, white ducks. To this day, a team picture in the high school yearbook portrays my submission. Gathered around the tennis net with rackets posed in hand is a team of regional champions dressed in the pure white of shorts, shirts, socks, and shoes. The co-captains stand proudly in the center, one dressed as a team member, the other looking like a throwback to the Don Budge era when shorts were taboo.

Fresher and hotter, I simmered and burned at the embarrassing episode of the week before. A year earlier I had withdrawn from the election as a shoo-in candidate for the vice-presidency of the Student Council when I learned that my responsibilities included leadership in planning for the Junior-Senior Prom. This year, however, the seniors had elected me a Class Historian. Elation surrounded the honor until I began to write the class history. When I realized that I must publicly report, "The Junior-Senior Prom; a good time was had by all," the facts of history conflicted with the goads of my conscience. How could I report a good time at a dance that I didn't attend? What would Brother Dan think when I read the history in public on Class Night? Having lost common sense and swallowing human pride, I wasted days on the struggle before I went to the Senior Class Advisor and resigned. When I told her the reasons, she answered like a Christian, "Everyone knows your convictions," she said, "Just state the facts like a reporter writing history. Everyone will understand." Relieved, I still left her office with the sheepish thought, "If this is what it means to lose your life for the sake of the Gospel, I'm not sure it's worth it." Just at the age when life should be a bundle of joy, I suffered from the torture of incidentals.

As Class Historian at Class Night, I followed with my Advisor's recommendation without guilt. But the dance was not over. My date for the evening was a high school junior named Betty. To complement her dark-haired beauty, Betty also had the distinction of holding the title as the Best Dancer in the high school, especially in the jitterbug. Despite my reputation as a non-dancer, Betty and I were identified as an "item" in the Class Prophecy with the prediction of a future together. After Class Night closed, Betty and I walked together into the lobby where a dozen or more senior classmates greeted us. At lead in the contingent was Noble, son of a noted automobile pioneer. Noble gave us a personal invitation to the dinner and dance hosted by his father at the Washtenaw Country Club. Noble invited us to attend with the backup of many voices. To say the least, I was conflicted. In the deepest part of my spirit, I wanted to go; but in the visible climate of my reaction, I could not make the decision. After repeated appeals from my classmates, Betty said to me, "If your parents don't want you to go, probably you shouldn't." On her word, I said "No" and we walked home, hand in hand in full formal dress, until we arrived at her home for a final goodnight kiss that sealed our respect forever.

****

Go back with me, then, to the cheap shot that Brother Dan enacted upon my soul. It turned into the last straw.

At home after the service, I found succor in the sympathy of Grandma McKenna. Fearless in her hindsight, she rued, "I wish that I had walked out. He was preaching against you and I knew it."

I, too, wished that she had walked out so that we could have died together. "What should I do?" I pondered aloud, "Call him?"

"Yes, you should," Grandma advised, "That's how the Bible says that Christians should handle their fights. But, before you do, let me tell you a story."

"When you were six months old, your folks lived in Sturgis, Michigan, along the bus line between Detroit and Chicago. Neither your mother or father knew Christ at the time. I, myself, was a new Christian as well as a new member of The Tabernacle. One night, a call came. Your mother was on the phone and weeping out of control. When I finally got her calmed down long enough to get the words out of her, she told me that you were not expected to live through the night. You had a childhood disease called 'erysipelas' that acted like a blood clot in the body. In your case, the clot had moved up your back and toward your heart." (Grandma momentarily lost her composure and began to weep). "If it turned that night into your heart, there was no hope. Your mother called me to ask if I would pray for a miracle. I prayed through the night for you, David. Sometime early in the morning, I fell asleep, but when I awakened, peace filled my soul and one thought occupied my mind. John Wesley once said that he became a 'brand snatched from the burning' when he was rescued from a burning home as a baby. In the same sense, I knew that you too were a brand snatched from the burning and that God had saved your life for a purpose."

The weight of divine destiny settled upon my soul.

"Do you know what happened?" Grandma McKenna continued, "The blood clot bypassed your heart, moved down your arm, and came out through the festering of your right thumb. Look at the thumbnail on your right hand. It's a double nail because you lost the first nail as a baby and it grew back that way. Never forget, David, that you are like John Wesley, 'a brand snatched from the burning.' God has a purpose for your life. Call him in the morning."

Early on New Year's Day, I phoned Brother Dan, "Hello, this is David McKenna," I began with a formal tone that hinted of things to come.

"Why, hello, Brother Dave, Hap . . . hap . . . happy New Year."

My mind reeled backward. How could he be so frivolous after what he said last night?

I stiffened with the answer, "Thanks. But I wanted to talk about something else."

"Sure, Brother Dave. You know that I am always ready to listen."

"YOU PREACHED AGAINST ME LAST NIGHT!" It had to be said that way for my relief and his attention.

"Why, Brother Dave, what gave you that idea?"

I spoke coldly now, "It was obvious. Who else is called to preach? Who else is going to Bible college? Who else is the Young People's leader?" Each question backed Brother Dan deeper into a corner.

"I still don't know what you mean. I only preach the truth . . . (pause) . . . *BUT, if the shoe fits, wear it.*"

Experience as a high school debater came to my aid, "Maybe the question is, 'What is Truth?' You said that I wasn't fit to be a preacher, go to Bible college, or lead the Young People's Society. Did you mean it?"

Brother Dan retreated behind a lie and a soft touch, "Oh, I didn't mean you. You know that you are the best Young People's President we have ever had. We're counting on you."

His crab walk inflamed me again, "Then why did you say what you did? Who else could you be talking about?"

Our strained conversation rose and fell for an hour. Without the protection of his pulpit, Brother Dan proved vulnerable—vacillating between preachy pronouncements and nervous attempts to laugh it off. Jab after jab, I caught him off guard. But he was master of the counterpunch and the coverup. When all else failed, he simply retreated behind the shield of his ministerial authority. So, at the sound the final bell, our bout ended in a draw. We hung up, not knowing at the time that we had put down the receiver on the cradle of communication for the rest of our natural lives. Never again did we exchange verbal blows; never again did we talk about the incident. Instead, we just walked away from each other until we went past shouting distance, formal contact, and almost past caring.

At first, I awaited judgment. When nothing happened, I turned into a bold, but silent, rebel. Brother Dan offered a "Let's forget it all" handshake at the Tabernacle door each Sunday morning. In return, I offered him half a smirk and half a smile that said, "I know the truth about you." By the time of high school graduation, I emotionally absented myself from every service. The final tie was cut on the last Sunday evening before I left for college. Mother rode with me to church in the four-wheel symbol of my new status as an 18-year-old who could own a 1933 Plymouth coupe, be drafted into the army, admitted to college, and tried for a crime in an adult court. Stopping at the railroad tracks just across from the Tabernacle, I turned to my mother and prophesied, "Mom, do you realize that this is my last night at church?"

Shocked and hurt, Mom pleaded, "Oh, son, don't say that." But I did and it was true. The next morning, I headed toward a Christian college and never looked back—until now.

****

As for the Tabernacle, dwindling crowds led to its heart-rending closure. The building still stands as a ghostly tribute to the humble members of the Body of Christ who found identity, meaning and the hope for salvation within its walls. Whatever their flaws, they were my first spiritual family. I loved them and they cared for me. Nor can I forget that it was in The Tabernacle that I first heard the Gospel, first felt the need for holiness, first heard the call to ministry, and first recognized that loyalty to God must take priority over human beings, no matter how dear.

As for Brother Dan, he preached until the woeful end and then traded his pulpit for the desk of a night clerk at a local hotel. A flashback reminded me that he was once my hero, resplendent in dress and gracious in demeanor, playing the trombone as smoothly as Tommy Dorsey and preaching the Word as fervently as Billy Sunday.

As for me, I left The Evangelistic Mission Tabernacle with my freedom as a flame and my faith as a thirst. Rather than living with the bitterness over the dubious demands of human holiness, I give thanks for the grace that saved my life as a baby and saved my soul as a youth.

In my first year of college, I took a course in Christian theology. When we came to the subject of Entire Sanctification or Holiness, the professor illustrated the doctrine by pulling a thread from his blue serge suit, stretching it up the light and saying,

> "Do you see? The thread from the suit has the text and tone of the whole cloth. So it is with us when we are sanctified. Every thread of our being will have the text and tone of the whole cloth of God's perfect will."

In that moment, my sanctifying moment, the beauty of holiness was restored and I was made whole.

Epilogue

THIS IS MY SONG

To be Read with Joy

Now for the rest of the story. Sixty years after writing this book, I now realize that the glimpses of grace that I saw through cracks in the jars of clay were actually threads of grace being woven into the whole cloth of God's will for my life. There are still knots on the underside of the cloth, but even they contribute to the tapestry of God's grace that is being woven on the topside.

Great grace has brought me to the age of 94 and retirement from a life-time ministry as pastor, chaplain, university and seminary president, and Christian author. Great grace has also prevented me from using my Tabernacle years as an excuse for rejecting the Church and its affiliations. I am a Free Methodist by love, a Wesleyan by choice, and an Evangelical by spirit.

Even greater grace has given me Janet, my beloved wife and partner in ministry for 73 years, and our four children, all of whom are devout Christians and leaders in their respective fields.

The greatest grace, however, is the evidence in my story that more than 80 years ago the Spirit of God vied with the judgment of man in the contest for my soul. Grace won and I now sing:

"O, for a thousand tongues to sing,

My great Redeemer's praise,
The glories of my God and King,
THE TRIUMPHS OF HIS GRACE!"

Amen and Amen.